The New Musi

Diane Hughes • Mark Evans • Guy Morrow • Sarah Keith

The New Music Industries

Disruption and Discovery

Diane Hughes
Macquarie University
Sydney, New South Wales, Australia

Guy Morrow
Macquarie University
Sydney, New South Wales, Australia

Mark Evans
University of Technology
Sydney, New South Wales, Australia

Sarah Keith
Macquarie University
Sydney, New South Wales, Australia

ISBN 978-3-319-82087-3   ISBN 978-3-319-40364-9 (eBook)
DOI 10.1007/978-3-319-40364-9

© The Editor(s) (if applicable) and The Author(s) 2016
Softcover reprint of the hardcover 1st edition 2016
This work is subject to copyright. All rights are solely and exclusively licensed by the Publisher, whether the whole or part of the material is concerned, specifically the rights of translation, reprinting, reuse of illustrations, recitation, broadcasting, reproduction on microfilms or in any other physical way, and transmission or information storage and retrieval, electronic adaptation, computer software, or by similar or dissimilar methodology now known or hereafter developed.
The use of general descriptive names, registered names, trademarks, service marks, etc. in this publication does not imply, even in the absence of a specific statement, that such names are exempt from the relevant protective laws and regulations and therefore free for general use.
The publisher, the authors and the editors are safe to assume that the advice and information in this book are believed to be true and accurate at the date of publication. Neither the publisher nor the authors or the editors give a warranty, express or implied, with respect to the material contained herein or for any errors or omissions that may have been made.

Cover illustration: © John Rawsterne / patternhead.com

Printed on acid-free paper

This Palgrave Macmillan imprint is published by Springer Nature
The registered company is Springer International Publishing AG
The registered company address is: Gewerbestrasse 11, 6330 Cham, Switzerland

FOREWORD

According to Charles Darwin's well-known theory, evolution is driven by 'survival of the fittest' (Darwin, 1859, p. 54). This does not necessarily mean the 'strongest' or the 'smartest'; 'the fittest' are those who can *adapt successfully* to an ever-changing world. Over the last 20 years digital technologies have been an 'extinction event' for many businesses that failed to adapt (for example, Polaroid, Blockbuster, Encyclopedia Britannica) while they have facilitated the rapid dominance of other new 'species' (for example, Instagram, Youtube, and Wikipedia). Schumpeter called this quasi-Darwinian process 'creative destruction' (Schumpeter, 1939), although the more specific and common term these days is 'digital disruption' (for example, Kusek & Leonhard, 2005; Collins & Young, 2014, p. 46; Homan, Cloonan, & Cattermole, 2016, p. 195).

Whatever name we choose, it is undeniable that the music industry has been disrupted severely by the last two decades of digital innovation. Some players have gone the way of the dinosaurs while others have adapted brilliantly.

This book considers these seismic shifts from multiple perspectives. After examining how and why things have changed it focuses primarily on the challenges and opportunities for musicians and music professionals seeking to build careers in the new digital world. What does it take not just to *survive*, but to *thrive*? Some consideration is also given to the consequences for educators seeking to prepare musicians and others for a future of continued flux.

The conclusions reached are of importance not just to those within the world of music but also arguably for those in other fields seeking to adapt to rapidly changing business environments. Music consumers tend to skew toward younger, tech-savvy 'early adopters' and a song requires relatively little bandwidth which means it can be distributed online more easily than a movie, television series or book. So in some respects the music industry has actually been a 'canary down the mine' for many other fields. Its various adaptation attempts over recent years may provide broader lessons in how—and how *not*—to operate in a post-industrial economy.

To some extent change has always been a constant for the music industry. Around a century ago wax cylinders and pianola rolls began to give way to shellac 78's as the dominant sound carriers of their day. From the 1950s jukeboxes loaded with 7" singles were supplanted by LPs and cassettes until, by 1995, over $25 billion worth of CDs were being sold globally each year. Nonetheless, the *pace*, *extent* and *direction* of change has increased markedly since that financial high water mark. Rampant online piracy and flawed supplier-centered MP3 solutions ushered in a period of track download dominance that is already being supplanted in most markets by streaming services like Spotify and Apple Music. After growing constantly for most of the twentieth century, real worldwide recording revenues are now roughly half what they were two decades ago.

Not only has music *consumption* changed, so have the means of music *discovery*. For most of the last century radio and television exposure were typically the key drivers of hit songs and while traditional media remains important, that discovery process is now vastly more fragmented. In some instances stars can emerge from just one online channel (namely, Shawn Mendes via Vine or Troye Sivan through YouTube), with Facebook and other forms of social media typically playing pivotal roles in exposing all new music. This space has even seen its own recent Darwinian struggles with services such as Napster, Friendster and Myspace roaring from obscurity to ubiquity and back again. In summary, change has become even more constant since the Internet began to take hold in the mid-1990s.

Of course all of this change has impacted hugely on the artists who make music. For the first half of the last century it was enough 'just' to have an evocative singing voice and to look compelling, although once the Beatles came along, 'real' artists were usually expected to write their own songs too. From the 1980s onwards the rise of MTV meant 'wannabe popstars' also typically had to be able to perform well in music videos, while over the last 20 years the list of 'job pre-requisites' has expanded significantly. New artists are now expected to be pithy linguists on Twitter, to have a knack for fascinating still photography (Instagram), and for writing, directing and performing in attention-grabbing short films for platforms including VEVO and Snapchat.

The bad news is that artists now need to do much more. The good news is that artists can do much more for themselves.

This is hugely liberating for motivated, diligent and highly creative people. In a bygone era of finite radio playlists and limited slots on TV variety shows most artists never even got a chance to be heard. A few 'middle of the road' performers usually enjoyed the most success precisely because they suited the handful of available channels that all sought to attract mass audiences. In the current era of virtually infinite bandwidth the opposite is often true—the middle of the road is now typically where artists get run over. Performers and/or their songs now often need to be toward the edges somehow in order to stand out. The work needs to be 'remarkable' in the sense of having some highly *unusual* qualities that move people to share it with friends.

As most artists are now 'broadcasting' (or narrowcasting) themselves constantly through their various online channels the main challenge is to break through the consequent clutter. This has been exacerbated by the democratization of recording and video production technology and the reduced need for physical distribution. In the twentieth century there were high barriers to entry for any artist seeking to be heard by a mass audience. Significant investment capital was needed to fund six-figure album and video budgets, and distribution infrastructure was required to keep LPs or CDs stocked in retailers around the world. Strong relationship networks with powerful media gatekeepers were also pivotal. All of these barriers to entry allowed record companies to assume a dominant role in most musical careers and meant that relatively few artists ever had their music heard by the general public.

These days, however, virtually every digital device contains recording and video editing software so almost anyone can create sound and vision for a tiny fraction of what it would have cost their parents at the same age. Today's artists can also immediately share and monetize their creativity with the world through any number of online outlets including Soundcloud, Beatport and YouTube so they often don't need access to a physical distribution network or to substantial seed capital (and even if they do need funding they may have the option of crowdsourcing it). The contemporary challenge for music makers and those who work with them is thus to create something so striking that it can make itself heard with, or without, early support from mainstream media. It's as simple, and as difficult, as that.

In short, most artists used to be trees falling in a forest with nobody to hear them. Now there are millions of 'trees' falling at once and so they need to create 'remarkable' things that allow them to be heard above a forest of digital din. Throw in increased competition from other emerging forms of entertainment—apps, games, video streaming etc—and the best possible advice for any beginner hoping to stand out from their virtually infinite musical peers is this: 'Don't. Be. Boring.'

As the above outline implies, digital disruption has transformed the relationship between artist, industry and consumer. Until quite recently music makers needed to somehow navigate their way past a series of industry gatekeepers—managers, talent scouts, promotion departments, radio programmers etc.—in order to eventually get a chance to be heard by most consumers. Along the way each of these gatekeepers relied largely on personal intuition and/or experience in deciding which artists to 'let past'. Career building was thus typically a *linear* process of charming and cajoling these gatekeepers. Consumers were only introduced at the final step when they were invited to choose from the small menu of songs funded by labels, programmed by radio or television stations and stocked by local retailers.

These days though the process is typically *circular*. The artist initially shares their music online with potential consumers. If that first exposure strikes a sufficiently strong chord then fans will start to share it widely. A blogger might notice that reaction and draw the song to the attention of more people. As a result of the consequent uptick in organic plays, the tune might be included on a widely heard Spotify playlist or receive its first spins on tastemaker radio stations. This upward spiral of artist-consumer-industry interactions can continue to unfold in many ways and at a dizzying pace where a 'remarkable' new song explodes from its first play to millions of plays within days. The key point is that the first steps are usually directly from artist-to-fan; most gatekeepers now typically *follow the fans* when it used to be the other way around.

We thus live in a world of 'build it and they will come[1]', with the still-coveted high rotation radio spins and magazine covers increasingly going to artists who have already proved online that their creations are made of the right stuff. This is bad news for anyone sitting around hoping some Svengali will swoop out of the clouds and make them a star, but it is fantastic news for hard-working artists who are keen to engage directly with their audience. It's also good news for music consumers who have more access to more music, more affordably than ever, but it's mixed news for the people who used to be gatekeepers.

This iterative discovery process obviously means that industry intermediaries no longer have to just back their instincts—instead they can support whatever is already generating an exponential adoption curve within their audience. As a result, garnering the support of such powerful people now typically depends on pointing to proof of early reactivity rather than on appeals to gut feel or longstanding relationships. The gatekeeper role has largely shifted from a seemingly omniscient picking of 'winners' to a role of enabling and amplifying audience 'likes'. Disintermediation has forced adaption. You are either genuinely adding value for artists and/or consumers or you are unfit to survive.

Incidentally this iterative discovery process is having profound impacts on the global spread of music. There are very few borders on the Internet and consequently Australian artists can now compete internationally on a more level playing field—largely free of the serious budgetary, geographical and institutional handicaps that confronted previous generations. Conversely this 'flatter' world presents serious issues for governments seeking to preserve local content quotas and for the nature of nineteenth century copyright laws in the twenty-first century. These are just a few of the many related issues you may wish to contemplate upon reading this book.

As this cursory consideration of the contemporary music industry landscape hopefully suggests, digital change has done lots of good but it has unavoidably created both winners and losers. Per Darwin's theory, the key in each case has been the willingness and ability to *adapt* by way of a series of 'variations' (Darwin, 1859, p. 54). Those who adapted best embraced the reality that musical careers hinge on the ability to strike a chord directly with an audience and to sustain that connection over time. When viewed in this way it is clear that while the *means* may have changed over recent decades, the *ends* really have not. The careers of successful artists, and those who work with them, have always depended on building large fanbases and that remains the 'main game'. However, artists no longer need to rely solely on powerful intermediaries to reach their audience. They can, and must, also speak authentically to fans directly through online channels.

Business school graduates might say that this is all simply about having a 'customer oriented mindset' (Lado, Paulraj, & Chen, 2011) and while that is probably true such a framing is unlikely to appeal to an artistic temperament. Thankfully the new ways of building connections with audiences can also be framed as creative opportunities. In fact most young musicians already do this intuitively for precisely that reason. The ability to express oneself in new ways online—as well as via songs—is now all just part of the appeal of a music career. Older readers seeking to understand these exciting artistic possibilities may like to consider what a young John, Paul, George and Ringo might have concocted with all these new digital tools at their fingertips.

Finally it's important to note that 'the music industry' is actually a variety of interconnected but largely separate types of businesses including recording, publishing, touring and merchandising. Digital disruption has altered all of them in various ways but it has had much greater impact on copyright-based enterprises (for example, record companies) than it has had on concert promoters, booking agents and suchlike because the live performance experience obviously cannot (yet?) be digitized.

Touring therefore actually remains the bedrock of most twenty-first-century musical careers. In a world of declining copyright revenues, live performances increasingly constitute the primary source of income for most artists, and global touring grosses continue to rise nearly every year. Gigging also remains one of the best ways of demonstrating audience reactivity and in this respect too, the more things change, the more things stay the same.

In the 1970s and 1980s heyday of Oz Rock one legendary record company mogul liked to say that his job was actually very easy: 'You just walk into a pub, you look to the left, you look to the right and if you can't see any walls because of all the sweaty punters then you sign the band'. In that respect, at least, little has changed, although this process is accelerated vastly online. Regardless of the means, an artist's ability to fascinate a sizable audience one way or another is still ultimately all that matters. The 'fittest' in the digital age will simply be those who adapt best to the new methods of creative self-expression and continue to find remarkable ways to strike a chord with fans. Despite all the digital disruptions, surviving in this new environment is clearly still more about evolution than revolution.

John Watson
President
John Watson Management/Eleven: A Music Company
http://elevenmusic.com

NOTES

1. A catchphrase from the popular film *Field of Dreams* (Phil Robinson, 1989).

References

Collins, S., & Young, S. (2014). *Beyond 2.0: The future of music*. Sheffield, UK: Equinox Publishing.
Darwin, C. (1859). *On the origin of species*. London: John Murray.
Homan, S., Cloonan, M., & Cattermole, J. (2016). *Popular music and the state: Policy notes*. London/New York: Routledge.
Kusek, D., & Leonhard, G. (2005). *The future of music: Manifesto for the digital music revolution*. Boston, MA: Berklee Press.
Lado, A. A., Paulraj, A., & Chen, I. J. (2011). Customer focus, supply-chain relational capabilities and performance: Evidence from US manufacturing industries. *The International Journal of Logistics Management, 22*(2), 202–221.
Schumpeter, J. (1939). *Business cycles: A theoretical, historical, and statistical analysis of the capitalist process*. New York: McGraw Hill.

Acknowledgements

We sincerely thank all our participants for their generosity and contributions to our project, and Dr Denis Crowdy for his contribution to the research.

We gratefully thank John Watson for his support in writing the Foreword to this volume.

We are also appreciative of the research assistance provided during the various stages of our research.

Contents

1	The State of Play	1
2	The New Business of Music	17
3	Standing Out in the Crowd	37
4	Creativities, Production Technologies and Song Authorship	63
5	The Realities of Practice	81
6	Popular Music Education	97
7	Conclusion: The 'New' Artist	117
Index		133

Notes on Authors

Mark Evans is Head of the School of Communication at the University of Technology, Sydney, Australia. Professor Evans is Series Editor for *Genre, Music and Sound* (Equinox Publishing) and is currently Editor for *The International Encyclopedia of Film Music and Sound*. He holds an Australian Research Council (ARC) grant to design an artistic and environmental map of the Shoalhaven basin in New South Wales, Australia.

Diane Hughes is Associate Professor in Vocal Studies and Music at Macquarie University, Australia. Her research areas include the singing voice, popular music pedagogy, film and sound, recording practices, the music industries, songwriting and the popular song. Associate Professor Hughes is currently the National President of the Australian National Association of Teachers of Singing Ltd.

Sarah Keith is a lecturer in Music and Media at Macquarie University, Australia. Dr Keith's research areas include popular music studies, Korean and Japanese popular music, other East Asian popular musics, the music industries, music and cultural policy, music and screen media, music and performance technologies, and computer-mediated composition.

Guy Morrow is a lecturer in Arts Industries and Management at Macquarie University, Australia. Dr Morrow focuses on understanding how artists are managed, both in terms of direct artist management and also through cultural policies. By examining the relationship between artists and managers, Dr Morrow generates core-related insights in the creative industries. He is currently the Secretary of the International Music Business Research Association.

List of Figures

Fig. 1.1	The creative continuum (Adapted from Madden & Bloom, 2001, pp. 413)	10
Fig. 2.1	360 model showing label intermediation between artists and audiences/fans	22
Fig. 2.2	Entrepreneur model showing the network of potential personnel and roles across the new music industries	24
Fig. 2.3	DIY model, showing that the artist bears the sole responsibility	25
Fig. 2.4	Linear model showing traditional intermediation between artist and fans	29
Fig. 2.5	Circular model encompassing artists, fans and industry	30
Fig. 6.1	An integrated music education model	107
Fig. 6.2	Artistry component	109
Fig. 6.3	Individualisation component	110
Fig. 6.4	Artist-entrepreneur component	112
Fig. 7.1	The new artist and engagement reciprocity	119

CHAPTER 1

The State of Play

Abstract The democratisation of music technologies and the digitisation of music practices have resulted in the development and fragmentation of related industries. No longer a label-centric industry, these new music industries facilitate increased opportunities for twenty-first century musicians to collaborate, to communicate and to interact with others interested in their music. This chapter introduces and identifies the new music industries, offers related definitions and outlines our research design and method.

Keywords Disruption • Discovery • Popular music • Creativities • Streaming

INTRODUCTION

There is no denying that massive disruption has come to the traditional music industry. From the chaos, and sometimes ashes, we have seen the birth of the new music industries (Williamson & Cloonan, 2007). The plurality is important here, for the democratisation of music technologies and the digitisation of music practices have resulted in the development and fragmentation of related industries. These industries offer possibilities for employment, 'success' and, most importantly, creativity to flourish. No longer a recording-dominated, label-centric industry, these new music industries facilitate increased opportunities for twenty-first century artists to collaborate, to communicate and to interact with others interested in

© The Editor(s) (if applicable) and The Author(s) 2016
D. Hughes et al., *The New Music Industries*,
DOI 10.1007/978-3-319-40364-9_1

their music. This brings with it many challenges for musicians and new terrains they must learn to navigate. This volume identifies aspects of the new music industries (for example, digital aggregators, social media consultants, online streaming sites), and considers how musicians, industry practitioners and audiences are locating themselves in this new landscape. Even traditional notions within the former music industry—performance, liveness, production, artist, training, success, creativity—have been altered through digital disruption. This book considers these fundamental changes, and seeks to equip participants of the new music industries with ideological and operational models of knowledge that will help them interact with the industries and their component parts. The strength of this volume lies in the ethnography that underpins it. Throughout the volume we document real narratives, from real people working in various corners of the new music industries. These voices tell the story of what is actually happening for musicians and industry professionals working in the disrupted environment. To highlight this, the volume is prefaced with the thoughts of John Watson. Watson, President of Eleven: A Music Company, is one of the leading industry voices in Australia and someone who has seen hundreds of narratives unfold (and change) before him. Watson provides real-world perspectives that effectively initiate the conversations that unfold throughout the rest of the volume. It is not the purpose of this volume to provide hypothetical theoretical positions, rather we focus on real-world stories from those at the coalface.

WHAT IS THE STATE OF PLAY?

As Watson notes in the Foreword to this volume, change has been a constant feature of the popular music industry, and that change has almost always been technologically driven. Indeed newness has been at the heart of musical development for centuries. Sometimes that newness has merely revolved around rejection of previous traditions: the romantic period's rejection of the perceived formulaic nature of classical music; bebop's rejection of the stable swing jazz that preceded it; or punk's rejection of the aesthetics of rock and pop. Other times newness has come through innovation, through avant-garde expressions of musicality: serialism's mathematical devotion to musical construction; *musique concrète*'s embrace of found sounds; or electronic dance music's commitment to entirely synthetic music composition. Newness and constant evolution are vital parts of music's history and future. What is different at this point in history is the pace of the change, and the extent of the change (see Watson, Foreword this volume). Change has come to the way music is produced (for example, studio, home, venue), distributed (for example, physical sales, online platforms) and consumed (for example, digital). And fundamental change has come to the business of music, so much so that it is now impossible to speak of a music industry in the singular. And ways into that business, even the manner of what success is (Hughes, Keith, Morrow, Evans, & Crowdy, 2013a), have changed forever. This has had huge effects on those who made, or sought to make a living through music. It also concerns regulators, advisory groups, government and music educators. The extent of the change is all-encompassing.

'Music piracy on a global level grew by 16.5% in the second half of 2015' (Reid, 2016). Such headlines have become commonplace in the last few years, as digital distribution creates digital consumption and allows complete circumvention of traditional business models. Reid's article reports on an anti-piracy study that surveyed 576 websites 'dedicated to music piracy, or contain[ing] significant music content' (Reid, 2016). The report found these sites had been visited over two billion times, with the top national offenders named (the USA coming in at number one). The extent of musical disruption can be seen in the globalized nature of it. Reid goes on to report that:

> It's already been proven in Norway and Sweden that better and more accessible streaming options help fight against piracy. A survey in December 2014 showed that just 4% of Norwegians under 30 still used illegal platforms to download music. Sweden's anti-piracy law, titled IPRED, resulted in increased music sales by 36% during the first six months of the law's implementation. (Reid, 2016)

Such tactics may well work for the developed world, but do nothing to combat the global piracy problem—if indeed one views piracy as a problem to be dealt with. What this shows us, however, is the speed of change and development. As the distribution avenues change and evolve, governments and regulators are forced to scramble for new solutions.

Part of that scramble has undoubtedly revolved around online streaming distribution and consumption patterns. While the Swedish and Norwegian examples cited above appear to be working to undermine piracy, how artists and their industry partners are remunerated and benefited through streaming services continues to be debated. A well-publicised example was when the band Atoms for Peace removed their music from the streaming site Spotify. The removal was pushed for by band member and long time Radiohead producer Nigel Godrich, who felt that Spotify and streaming sites in general were not going to help the development of new music (Bychawski, 2013). He was dubious that smaller producers and artists would receive any significant payments from streaming, but that major labels would still prosper:

> The way that Spotify works is that the money is divided up by percentage of total streams. Big labels have massive back catalogues so their 40 year old record by a dead artist earns them the same slice of the pie as a brand new track by a new artist. The big labels did secret deals with Spotify and the like in return for favourable royalty rates. The massive amount of catalogue being streamed guarantees that they get the big massive slice of the pie (that $500 million) and the smaller producers and labels get pittance for their comparatively few streams. This is what's wrong. (Godrich, cited in Bychawski, 2013)

Similarly, Taylor Swift pulled her catalogue from Spotify very publicly in 2014. Given her net worth—according to Forbes she made US$80 million in 2015—it would have been nonsensical to complain about how little money she was receiving from the service. Rather she tied her argument to issues of artistic value.

> With Beats Music and Rhapsody you have to pay for a premium package in order to access my albums. And that places a perception of value on what I've created. On Spotify, they don't have any settings, or any kind of qualifications for who gets what music. I think that people should feel that there is a value to what musicians have created, and that's that. (Swift cited in Engel, 2014)

Audiences and fans will increasingly be drawn into this debate of what art, in this case musical product, should cost. And the lines of division are beginning to be demarcated, with huge levels of illegal downloading still occurring, alongside increasing numbers of successful crowdsourcing campaigns, where fans are giving directly to the artist. The business of streaming services will continue to be an added complication within this landscape, but in pure distribution terms they offer artists another avenue to be heard, and heard widely at that. Increasingly, there is no illusion about the take-up from the public:

> Subscription services, part of an increasingly diverse mix of industry revenue streams, are going from strength to strength. Revenues from music subscription services—including free-to-consumer and paid-for tiers—grew by 51.3 per cent in 2013, exceeding US$1 billion for the first time and growing consistently across all major markets. (IFPI, 2014, p. 7)
>
> Record companies and chart compilers are increasingly adapting charts to reliably reflect the popularity of an artist's music in the streaming world.

It has also become more common to use streaming data to calculate Gold and Platinum awards certifications around the world. (IFPI, 2015, p. 13)

Another aspect of the distribution problem is the more basic one of getting your music heard (see also Watson, Foreword this volume). As we will document later, it is not enough to record your song and put it online; more needs to happen to get it 'heard' by people. One industrial change that has become a prominent part of solving this is the rise of synchronisation (the combination of an audio text with an image text, most notably in film, television or video games). Television synchronisation, while not a new phenomenon, is probably the most notable here. Long the most denigrated media form for audio, the impact of a high-profile sync (synchronisation) can now break an artist, or resurrect a flailing career. Evidence of this can be seen in articles such as 'Billboard's First-Ever TV's Top Music Power Players List Revealed' (Billboard, 2015), which highlights the audience numbers and earning potential for artists with high-impact syncs.

Performance outlets have always been important for musicians, and with the diminishing returns from recorded output, performance is becoming the dominant revenue stream for artists. But performance venues are subject to seasonal variances in government policy and other regulatory aspects that can impinge on artist opportunities to perform. In February 2014, the New South Wales government introduced 'lockout' laws into some areas of the Sydney CBD. The new laws include a 1.30am lockout (effectively stopping patrons entering venues after this time) and 3am last drinks. The laws were part of the state government's crackdown on drug and alcohol-fuelled violence. While social benefits are evident, there have been some severe side-effects for the city's performance culture. Between 31 January 2013 and 1 February 2015, collection agency APRA-AMCOS reported a 40% drop in ticket sales to live performance venues, along with a '19 per cent decline in attendances across all live venues over the same period and a 15 per cent fall in the amount venues spent on live performers' (Vincent, 2016). Live Music Office policy director John Wardle stated: 'These figures demonstrate the actual impacts for musicians, venues, businesses. People are looking at this closely to try and find a way through because they are going out of business' (cited in Vincent, 2016). While this is a localised example,[1] the point here is the sudden change to an established culture. Artists may have prepared their performance strategy around late-night gigs, only to have it wrecked by forces beyond their control. As Wardle pointed out, 'The music industry had no time to prepare so the impacts were greater than they might have been' (cited in Vincent, 2016). Such events are hard for artists to plan for—though, as will be seen, the ability to adapt and be flexible is a key competency in the new music industries.

Disruption and Discovery

As noted in the subtitle, this book is concerned with notions of disruption and discovery in the new music industries. There is much written about the disruption side of things (for example, Kusek & Leonhard, 2005; Collins & Young, 2014, p. 46; Homan, Cloonan, & Cattermole, 2016, p. 195) and it was a key issue for our research participants, but there is plenty of discovery going on as well. Artists are learning how to adapt into the new territories, how to create new roles for themselves and their teams, and most importantly, how to develop new models for creative practices and business management. Thus for all the disruption thrust on the sector, surviving and/or prospering in the new world *is* more about evolution than revolution (Watson, Foreword this volume). Artists are being required to adapt their involvement with all facets of the music industries, to evolve alongside technological development. As digital access broadens for all participants, so artists must discover new ways of interacting with audiences, producing content, and engaging with industry figures. It is an evolution that remains full of promise despite the move away from of record label-centric models. The move to a do-it-yourself (DIY) model necessitates the evolution of new skills. Previously some of these skills had been in the possession of professionals in other industries, but in other cases they are brand-new capabilities evolving alongside the technology that makes them possible. For some, this is still a utopian view of the age of artist-entrepreneurship. They argue that traditional music industry intermediaries remain essential for artist survival (Hesmondhalgh & Meier, 2015). Our research throughout this volume shines a light on those evolving their creativities for the digital age, and turning their back on traditional models of success and associated revenue.

Owing to our focus on discovery and disruption, this is not a book about policy. Our book is grounded in the practice of artists, industry practitioners and, of course, fans. There have been several recent studies providing useful insights into the changing nature, or the need of change, in policy directions within the new musical industries. Most pertinently, Homan, Cloonan and Cattermole's (2015) recent volume has broad concerns about policy across three nation states:

We are interested in the effect of policies—their impacts upon musicians, fans, managers, corporations, built environments—and in their histories, rationales and formations... Public funding for pop music has historically stood in the shadow of funding for art music. We will consider here how this is changing and address the shifting nature of state intervention, examining in particular forms of policy other than funding models. (pp. 2–3)

Such a volume sits alongside our practice-grounded study, highlighting the external forces that are coming to bear on everyday practitioners and creativities.

Certainly there are issues aplenty for governments and regulators as a result of digital disruption. While the economic ramifications of the new business flows (the loss of sales tax or import tax, for instance) are readily identifiable, other, less tangible implications are becoming more apparent. The flatter world created through digital production and distribution complicates attempts to enforce local content quotas and protect local industries and artists. The whole enforcement of copyright, a largely historical concept and set of laws, is immeasurably more difficult in the twenty-first century. Homan et al. (2015) feel that the broader agenda of copyright reform has been clouded by the jockeying to keep up with contemporary (read digital) infringements:

The enormous effort in drafting new laws on copyright infringement has certainly overshadowed other important aspects of copyright law and, more importantly, how it operates more broadly within national contexts. (p. 117)

But, as Watson notes in the Foreword to this volume, there are vast opportunities and areas of discovery in all of this. There are no absolute borders on the Internet. Governments might be scrambling to appropriately regulate and get recompensed for artistic endeavor, but there is nothing (in practical terms) to stop a rapper from a small regional area becoming a global phenomenon. There is little to stop the music of one region reaching another corner of the Earth. However, as we will detail later in the volume, the power structures behind the new music industries still yield considerable power. The opportunities are there but the battle remains to have your music heard.

Definitions

Many of the terms and concepts in this volume are familiar to a wide audience. However, great differences exist in the way terminology is employed. Often in the new music industries terms have been reappropriated and are used in contexts very different from their original formation. One recurring notion that features throughout the volume is that of the artist. For our purposes we have restricted its use to musical artists only, including bands, solo musicians, producers and so forth. We acknowledge that there are many personnel involved in crafting a musical career (for example, stylists, managers, social media strategists), however our definition of an artist is restricted to those involved in musical creation. In line with the new musical industries our use recognises the diversity of musical creativities and roles now present. We delineate the other industry practitioner roles, and normally stipulate exactly the participant role/s involved (in brackets) throughout the volume.

One longstanding issue with the term artist revolves around professionalism. At what point is an artist considered a professional? With the new impetus on DIY creation and dissemination in the new music industries, this question is even further clouded. In their 2010 study into the economics of professional artists, Throsby and Zednik (2010) usefully note that:

> In some fields, the definition of a professional is straightforward... For artists, any single test is inadequate as a comprehensive definition of professional standing. Criteria that are used in other occupations may or may not apply; for example, an income test is unsatisfactory since in a given year a professional artist may earn little or no income, while a test based on formal qualifications will overlook professional artists who are self-taught... a primary concern for our definition of professionalism relates to the manner and standards of an artist's work—is he or she working at a level of work and degree of commitment appropriate to the norms for professional recognition in their particular artform? (p. 14)

While useful, where this explanation struggles is in relation to the 'norms for professionalism' in the current environment. As will be shown, it could now be normal for an artist to operate outside of any formal industrial apparatus and construct their own career entirely on their own. Yet within Throsby and Zednik's (2010) schema this still involves a degree of commitment that is often extraordinary. Other artists may seek to reach a wide audience with their music, but this might occur through traditional performance, or synchronization, or online distribution. To that end, even the concept of success has changed (Hughes et al., 2013a). Measures of success have broadened from traditional ideas of record sales, peer awards and performance venue sizes to include reach, personal contentment and artistic integrity (see, for example, Letts, 2013). Global pop phenomenon Sia (Furler) is an example. Having crafted a solo career since 1997, finally achieving global success with hits such as 'Clap Your Hands' (written by Furler and Dixon, released 2010) and 'Chandelier' (written by Furler and Shatkin, from the chart-topping *1000 Forms of Fear* album released through Inertia/Monkey Puzzle/RCA, 2014), her well-publicized attempts at performance anonymity have coupled with a desire to write songs for others, rather than be the focal point herself: 'I don't care about commercial success,' she says. 'I get to do what I love and communicate whatever I want' (Sia cited in Gallo, 2013).

Popular music success has long been concerned with the idea of reaching an audience, and preferably having them buy recorded music (Shuker, 1994; Longhurst, 1995). Yet notions of fandom, or active audiences, have also been developed for many years (Negus, 1996). In the current climate we see an even more overt separation between the two descriptors. An audience for your music is viewed as a broad collective, a faceless, numberless group that will engage with your music at some minor level (perhaps merely by hearing it on a Pandora playlist). Fans in the new music industries are extremely active. They might undertake 'work' for you on social media, reposting announcements of new products or video clips, they could circulate information about upcoming gigs, and of course, they provide direct feedback to artists. Fans more than ever are active agents. They are, however, potentially coming from all directions and, in this sense, are unpredictable. They are invested in the work of the artist, and in terms of crowdsourcing, might even be contributing funds to help support the work of the artist. There is no doubt that, in the context of the new music industries, the question of who decides what is novel and creative is dependent on a social system that has been broadened by social media: fans decide at the outset of the artist's career whether they deem the music to be novel/creative. Moreover, they make judgments about the ethos of the artist, their musical integrity, and their capacity for self-identification. Throughout this volume, the terms audience and fans are used carefully and contextually, referencing the different levels of engagement present.

CREATIVITIES

We make mention of the (new) creativities unpinning the music industries. Again, we prefer the term *creativities* (after Burnard, 2012) to denote a range of creative options (both musical and business) and refer to *creativity* in the singular in relation to the creative process. In the new music industries, understanding a continuum of creativities is particularly helpful in delineating artist endeavour. Madden and Bloom (2001) posited 'hard' and 'weak' creativity in order to aid clarity around the way creativity was being deployed (p. 412). For them:

> 'Hard' creativity represents the creation of something that is 'brand new' in the sense that it is unprecedented (creation as invention). 'Weak' creativity represents something merely being 'brought into being' (creation simply as production). Hard and weak creativity are clearly not opposite ends of a spectrum, but have a subset/superset relationship. It is useful, therefore, to introduce a third form to contrast directly with hard creativity. This form will be called 'soft' creativity, and taken to represent reproduction, i.e. completely non-inventive production... In practice, creative acts will inevitably involve some mix of hardness and softness, and will therefore be positioned somewhere inside the limits of the hard–soft continuum. (Madden & Bloom, 2001, pp. 412–413)

In terms of our discussion of the new music industries, we address this continuum of creativities by discussing soft creativity, reproduction, standardisation and uniformity in Chapter 2, and hard creativity, innovation and novelty in Chapter 3. Undeniably, being able to view the continuum of creativities is essential to artists. At different times they might employ different strategies to build audience engagement or creative exposure in different continuum contexts. The diagram shows the continuum, and how it pertains to material covered in different chapters of the volume (Fig. 1.1).

It might appear that the words used in this continuum have a pejorative element; they do not. Standardisation and uniformity might be entirely fitting for a covers band (see Homan, 2006) that is minimising their own hard creative input in order to faithfully replicate a sound or experience for an audience. They might even use this vehicle to help develop some hard

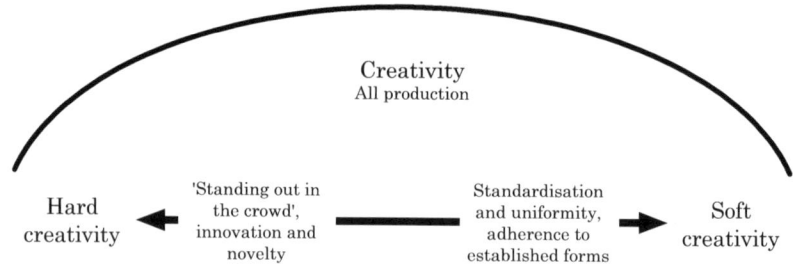

Fig. 1.1 The creative continuum (Adapted from Madden & Bloom, 2001, pp. 413)

creativity (see Chapter 4). Hence the continuum is quite fluid. What is important is artists positioning themselves within it, understanding which direction they are taking their craft and for what purpose. Interestingly, both ends of the continuum can yield substantial financial success, so neither should be considered inferior to the other. In terms of success, especially in light of the changing definitions of artist success (see Hughes et al., 2013a), both can produce rewarding levels of success. In light of these observations we have adapted the model to include soft creativity (rather than weak, which has other connotations). As will be shown, this becomes a useful frame for the research presented throughout this volume.

RESEARCH RATIONALE AND DESIGN

Disruption in industrial practices, changes in accessibility and distribution, and the democratisation of technologies, challenge the traditional career development model associated with the label-centric music industry. While the literature identifies aspects of the resultant industries afforded *by* and *through* digital disruption, there is a paucity of detailed accounts of the impact of resultant changes on career development and lived experiences. Our research is significant, as it addresses this gap and extrapolates new and emerging career pathways in ways that have implications and considerations for best practice, career models, the health and wellbeing of sector workers, music education, and the interaction of music industries with government policies and procedures.

The research underpinning this volume investigated the contributory factors and influences (including technological ones) on career development in new music industries. With the aim of identifying new and evolving career trajectories, models and strategies, our research targeted music practices and practitioners. We addressed the primary research questions: (1) What are the new music industries? (2) What constitutes career development within these industries? (3) How do artists manage career development and/or a sustainable trajectory within the new industries?

The research team brought together investigators with a range of expertise. Our team was comprised of experienced practitioners in several areas of music including music production, artist development, music education and artist management. At the outset, we had a choice of a broad-based survey design or a more in-depth approach. We choose the latter in order to engage with participants in ways that allowed for meaningful and, at times, lengthy discussion. Our resultant ethnographic design involved qualitative data collection (focus groups and semi-structured interviews) together with attendance at peak Australian industry conferences including BIGSOUND (Brisbane),[2] Face the Music (Melbourne) and the Electronic Music Conference (Sydney) that added ethnographic context to our research. Our project was funded by a Macquarie University Research Development Grant (2012–2014) and approved as being compliant with the National Statement on Ethical Conduct in Human Research.[3]

The research for this volume was necessarily conducted in Australia, however, what we are dealing with are the new global musical industries. The simultaneous individualisation and interconnectedness of the digital industries means that commonalities exist across countries and regions. The following methodological structure outlines Australian-based activities, yet the narratives and examples collected are being replicated around the world. The disruption and discovery documented throughout this volume are not exclusive to Australian markets.

The research design was comprised of four stages. Stage 1[4] involved a comprehensive review of the literature covering aspects of industry that included digital disruption, traditional music industry roles and expectations, contemporary music education, and music technologies. Drawing on our analysis of the literature and previous research studies, we developed questions for Stages 2 and 3.

Seven focus groups, of approximately 2 hours duration each, were undertaken in Sydney (×3), Melbourne (×2), and Brisbane (×2). These specific cities were selected as primary locations of employment within the new music industries in Australia; they respectively represented the three eastern states of New South Wales (NSW), Victoria and Queensland where a substantial amount of work in the music industries is typically negotiated that may be undertaken elsewhere in the country. Furthermore, many artists living and working in other Australian jurisdictions have associated agents, managers, labels and publishers located in these three states. These states are identified areas of musical employment (Australian Bureau of Statistics, 2008), with more people employed in the categories of 'Music Publishing' and 'Music and other sound recording activities' than elsewhere in Australia. Each focus group represented a diverse range of sector workers from artists through to digital strategists and music publishers. The topics covered in each group included: (1) the new music industries and the ways in which these industries have changed/evolved, (2) career development within these industries, (3) technological developments including production aesthetics and associated skill sets, and (4) considerations and implications for navigating the new industries. A total of twenty-one participants and five researchers took part in the focus groups.

Stage 3 in-depth interviews were undertaken with participants who were purposively sampled to target specific areas of investigation that emerged through our analysis of Stage 1 data. Again, interviews were undertaken in Sydney, Melbourne and Brisbane, although interviewees themselves were drawn from across the country. During this stage we engaged primarily with artists, and with industry practitioners associated with artist development and/or the realities of practice. The areas for investigation included: (1) determining roles and strategies in the new music industries, (2) new and emerging industry practices and/or technologies, (3) developments and changes, (4) considerations and implications, (5) future directions, and (6) real-world advice. A constant comparative method of analysis was used to identify similarities and differences in the participant perspectives. A total of nineteen participants and four researchers took part in these in-depth interviews.

Our participant voices (from Stages 2 and 3) are heard and quoted throughout this volume. These participant voices provide rich empirical data reflective of real-world events and experiences. Participants are denoted by their names and role (in brackets), and are distinguished from other cited quotations as, being previously unpublished, they are not included in our reference list.

During the final stage of our project, we consolidated and reported our findings in various formats. We presented our initial findings at an industry symposium hosted at Macquarie University, Sydney, Australia.[5] Here, we discussed a detailed framework of the new music industries for stakeholders and our research participants. Further reporting on our findings has included national and international presentations, and peer-reviewed publications (Hughes et al., 2013a; Hughes, Keith, Morrow, Evans, & Crowdy, 2013b; Hughes, Evans, Keith, & Morrow, 2014). Our cumulative findings are presented in this volume. The primary aim of the research that informs our findings was to explore how disruption and discovery have combined to create new opportunities for artists. The next chapter of this volume starts by considering how the relationships between artists, managers and labels have changed in the post-digital music industries. Watson's observation (see Foreword this volume) that artist careers have shifted from being linear to circular draws attention to the shifting gatekeepers, milestones, and goals in artists' careers today. Whereas known entities such as labels and broadcasters once constituted the foundation of music industry, today's environment is much more opaque and revenue streams are much less certain. The following chapter examines various approaches artists can take to negotiate this terrain, proposing three career models of operation for artists in the new musical industries. These models go on to provide the foundation for subsequent chapters, and their analyses of prizes and pitfalls of the new conditions for artists.

Notes

1. Although it is soon to be replicated in Brisbane's Fortitude Valley, a hub of musical performance venues in the city.
2. BIGSOUND, for example, is a QMusic Project. It is an annual conference that hosts keynotes, panels and showcases (BIGSOUND, 2014). QMusic is an association in the state of Queensland Australia that focuses on music industry development (QMusic, 2014).
3. Ethics approval to conduct the research was secured from Macquarie University Human Research Ethics on 15 October, 2012.
4. Our investigation began in November 2012 and concludes with this volume.
5. The research symposium *Trajectories in the New Music Industries* featured a range of presentations by each member of the research team, and included invited speakers and performers. The symposium was held on 27 June 2014.

References

Australian Bureau of Statistics. (2008). *Employment in culture – Australia – 2006*. Retrieved April 4, 2012, from http://www.ausstats.abs.gov.au/ausstats/subscriber.nsf/0/6A0842636FC03C4CCA2573FB000BCD2D/$File/62730_2006.pdf

Billboard. (2015). *Billboard's first-ever TV's top music power players list revealed*. Retrieved March 2, 2016, from http://www.billboard.com/articles/business/6699790/tv-music-power-players-list-2015

BIGSOUND. (2014). 10–12 Sept 2014/Brisbane Australia. Retrieved on December 10, 2014, from http://www.qmusic.com.au/bigsound/2014/

Burnard, P. (2012). *Musical creativities in practice*. Oxford: Oxford University Press.

Bychawski, A. (2013). *Atoms for Peace's Nigel Godrich: 'I'm not bitching about not getting paid'*. Retrieved March 2, 2016, from http://www.nme.com/news/atoms-for-peace/71462

Collins, S., & Young, S. (2014). *Beyond 2.0: The future of music*. Sheffield, UK: Equinox Publishing.
Engel, P. (2014). Taylor Swift explains why she left Spotify. Retrieved March 2, 2016, from http://www.businessinsider.com.au/taylor-swift-explains-why-she-left-spotify-2014-11
Gallo, P. (2013). Sia: The Billboard cover story. Retrieved February 5, 2016, from http://musicinaustralia.org.au/index.php/Survey_of_Successful_Contemporary_Musicians
Hesmondhalgh, D., & Meier, L. (2015). Popular music, independence and the concept of the alternative in contemporary capitalism. In J. Bennett & N. Strange (Eds.), *Media independence* (pp. 94–116). Abingdon, UK/New York: Routledge.
Homan, S. (Ed.). (2006). *Access all eras: Tribute bands and global pop culture*. Maidenhead, UK: Open University Press.
Homan, S., Cloonan, M., & Cattermole, J. (2015). *Popular music and cultural policy*. Abingdon, UK/New York: Routledge.
Homan, S., Cloonan, M., & Cattermole, J. (2016). *Popular music and the state: Policy notes*. London/New York: Routledge.
Hughes, D., Evans, M., Keith, S., & Morrow, G. (2014). A 'duty of care' and the professional musician/artist. In G. Carruthers (Ed.), *Proceedings of the commission for the education of the professional musician (CEPROM)* (pp. 31–41). Brazil: Belo Horizonte.
Hughes, D., Keith, S., Morrow, G., Evans, M., & Crowdy, D. (2013a). What constitutes artist success in the Australian music industries? *International Journal of Music Business Research (IJMBR)*, 2(2), 60–80.
Hughes, D., Keith, S., Morrow, G., Evans, M., & Crowdy, D. (2013b). Music education and the contemporary, multi-industry landscape. In *Redefining the musical landscape: Inspired learning and innovation in music education XIX ASME National Conference Proceedings* (pp. 94–100). Brisbane, Australia.
IFPI (International Federation of Phonographic Industry). (2014). *Digital music report 2014*. Retrieved January 9, 2015, from http://www.ifpi.org/downloads/Digital-Music-Report-2014.pdf
IFPI (International Federation of Phonographic Industry). (2015). *Digital music report 2015*. Retrieved December 4, 2015, http://www.ifpi.org/downloads/Digital-Music-Report-2015.pdf
Kusek, D., & Leonhard, G. (2005). *The future of music: Manifesto for the digital music revolution*. Boston, MA: Berklee Press.
Letts, R. (2013). Survey of successful contemporary musicians, music in Australia knowledge base. Retrieved March 1, 2016, from http://musicinaustralia.org.au/index.php/Survey_of_Successful_Contemporary_Musicians
Longhurst, B. (1995). *Popular music and society*. Cambridge, UK: Polity Press.
Madden, C., & Bloom, T. (2001). Advocating creativity. *International Journal of Cultural Policy*, 7(3), 409–436.

Negus, K. (1996). *Popular music in theory: An introduction*. Cambridge, UK: Polity Press.
QMusic. (2014). *About us*. Retrieved December 10, 2014, from http://www.qmusic.com.au/?contentID=620
Reid, P. (2016). Music piracy up 16% worldwide. *The Music Network*. Accessed 4 March, 2016, from https://www.themusicnetwork.com/news/music-piracy-up-16-worldwide
Shuker, R. (1994). *Understanding popular music*. London: Routledge.
Throsby, D., & Zednik, A. (2010). *Do you really expect to get paid? An economic study of professional artists in Australia*. Melbourne: Australia Council for the Arts.
Vincent, P. (2016). Sydney lockout laws bite as live music ticket sales crash. *Brisbane Times*. Retrieved February 29, 2016, from http://www.brisbanetimes.com.au/entertainment/music/sydney-lockout-laws-bite-as-live-music-ticket-sales-crash-20160218-gmxgot.html
Williamson, J., & Cloonan, M. (2007). Rethinking the music industry. *Popular Music, 26*(2), 305–322.

CHAPTER 2

The New Business of Music

Abstract This chapter outlines three career models—360, Entrepreneur and DIY—identified as being significant and viable models within the new industries. The functions and variations of each model are discussed, together with associated revenue streams and risk factors. The chapter discusses traditional *linear* career development and introduces the concept of new *circular* career development identified within the new music industries. The differences between traditional and non-traditional career models conclude the chapter.

Keywords New music industries • 360 • Entrepreneur • DIY • Circular

This chapter expands upon the notion that career development has evolved from being *linear* to *circular* (see Watson, Foreword this volume). By describing this new circular process, the chapter addresses contemporary strategies for the business practices of the new music industries, and identifies pragmatic issues for the new musician. It outlines a variety of career trajectories, and suggests that, through a circular process, major record labels are devolving risk through neoliberal[1] restructuring. In addition, it argues that there is still 'standardisation and uniformity' (McGuigan, 2010, p. 329) in many sectors of the industries[2]. This is because soft artistic creativity is evident within the new business of music (see Fig. 1.1), and in the context of these industries, major record labels have become more reactive. Our argument is that artists are responding to this reactivity with multiple creativities (both soft and hard and various combinations of the two). While the next chapter will focus on hard creativity and innovation, the models we introduce in this chapter inevitably involve a mix of hardness and softness. In terms of soft artistic creativity, our argument in this chapter is that many artists (and their management teams if they have them) are embracing standardisation and uniformity in order to directly attract audiences, to demonstrate exponential growth to potential investors (i.e. major record labels) and to manage the financial risk they themselves must take in order to get their career started.

This chapter highlights different models for navigating the new music industries, such as the 360 (label) model, the entrepreneur model, and the do-it-yourself (DIY) model. In particular, our research identifies that the DIY model is a significant, viable, and even fundamentally necessary model within the new music industries, particularly for emerging artists. However, no one model is offered as an either/or option. For example, an artist may start out by managing their own career (the DIY model), but will then operate in a way that is in line with the entrepreneur model as more service providers become involved. In order to further grow an audience/fanbase, the artist may then work with a record label under a 360 deal (the 360 model). The artist may also navigate back through these models if a label relationship ceases. While the combination of models and trajectories would evolve and devolve over time, artists may also simultaneously work under a combination of models across different geographic territories.

REVENUE STREAM GROUPS

There are five main revenue stream groups that allow income to be generated from popular music: *live performance, merchandise, song publishing, recorded music* and *sponsorship deals* (Morrow, 2006). Other more marginal streams include grants and funding, as well as miscellaneous income streams such as workshops and teaching. The term 'revenue stream groups' is used throughout this volume as it enables the alignment of associated income streams. This alignment is highlighted, for example, in relation to song publishing:

> The music publishing industry earns its money by exploiting the copyright in music and lyrics. There are a number of significant income streams within

this revenue stream group that include royalties received from pressing records and CDs ('mechanical royalties'), public performance, broadcast and cablecast ('performance royalties'), sale of printed music ('print royalties'), use of music with visual images, e.g. film, TV programs and adverts, 'synchronisation royalties'), use of music in theatre and ballet ('grand rights royalties'), ringtones and downloads. (Morrow, 2006, pp. 93–94)

While revenue stream groups are not new concepts, emergent trends in the new industries (for example, the growth in revenue generated through online digital strategies) are seen to shift the relevance of streams within the groups. Globally, the digital revenue stream, for example, now accounts for approximately 39% of recorded music revenues (IFPI, 2014, p. 6). In Australia, digital revenues overtook the physical sales revenue stream for the first time in 2013 and represented 54.7% of the total revenue in this group (Australian Recording Industry Association, 2014). Other markets have shown an even greater shift towards digital formats—for example, Nordgård (2016) noted that:

> The market share of on-demand music streaming services in Norway exceeded 75 per cent in 2014, hence placing it together with a handful of countries that can be considered pioneers in this space. (p. 175)

Interestingly, in terms of recent developments in the recorded music revenue group, countries such as Sweden have embraced the digital transition to online streaming with subscription streaming services accounting for 84% of Swedish digital revenues during the first 10 months of 2011 (IFPI, 2011). This level of adaptation is testimony to the evolutionary nature of this particular revenue stream group. As new music consumption habits continue to be adopted in greater numbers, a commercially viable future for this revenue stream group may lie ahead:

> Music subscription services were a major driver of digital growth, sustaining a sharp upward trend of recent years. Revenues rose 39.0 per cent in 2014 to US$1.57 billion. Revenues from music subscription services now make up 23 per cent of digital revenues globally, up from only 18 per cent in 2013. (IFPI, 2015, p. 6)

Music subscription services have seen the number of users who pay for the service grow steadily in recent years, with an estimation that '41 million people worldwide now pay for a music subscription service'

(IFPI, 2015, p. 6). Rather than solely focusing on the recorded music revenue stream, it is important to consider career sustainability and to recognise the different and possible revenue stream groups. In this way, a holistic view of the music business that accounts for the new industries is possible. Although the data relating to increasing revenue from music subscription services is promising, the recognition of the five main revenue stream groups has been brought into sharper focus in recent times. This is particularly relevant given that the recording industry lost approximately half of its exchange value[3] over the fifteen-year period between 1996 and 2011 (IFPI, 2011). Therefore, rather than simply focusing on the role of record companies, this chapter outlines the need for a more inclusive view of the music industries incorporating all five key revenue stream groups.

The multiplicity of, and developments in, key revenue stream groups has direct relevance to the proliferation of the new music industries as no one singular industry or practice underpins all revenue stream groups. The research of Williamson and Cloonan (2007) highlights two main problems with the term 'music industry'[4]:

> First, it suggests a homogenous industry, whereas the reality is of disparate industries with some common interests. Secondly, the term is frequently used synonymously with the recording industry. Thus the term 'the music industry' is often used in ways that lead to misrepresentation and confusion. It suggests simplicity where there is complexity and homogeneity where there is diversity. (p. 305)

Williamson and Cloonan also note that the use of the singular 'music industry' term serves vested interests, such as those pertaining to recording industry associations (p. 306). Thus, we use the term 'music industries'. In particular, we consider the different industries that stem from the five key revenue stream groups.

Career Models

The three models identified in our research—the 360 model, the Entrepreneur model, and the DIY model—are not offered here as either/or options as none were identified as being immutably fixed in any one career trajectory. We provide a series of models for navigating the new music industries that may be representative of different career stages and trajectories. Each model carries a different level of potential risk (financial and artistic) that is discussed below.

The 360 Model (Model 1)

This model arose as labels sought to gain larger returns drawn from a broader range of potential revenue streams. Its implementation is significant because since the arrival of the Internet and the development of digital music strategies, international recorded music revenues had fallen from over USD $40 billion in 2000 (Leyshon, Webb, French, Thrift, & Crewe, 2005) to USD $15 billion in 2013 (IFPI, 2014). In response to revenue decline and disruption more broadly, record labels began employing a more holistic view of the artist's career and the potential product/s associated with it. The 360-degree (or '360') deal emerged and involves a record label participating in all five revenue stream groups.

According to Goodman (2010), in 2007 Warner Music Group (WMG) made 360-degree participation in its artists' income streams company policy. The 360 deals meant that '20 percent of Atlantic and Warner Bros. Records A&R budgets would be spent on 360 deals' (Goodman, 2010, p. 257). Under what became known as their Collateral Entertainment Agreement (CEA), Goodman noted:

> ... they were arguing that even as sales fell, records drove a career and made all other opportunities possible, and that in order to continue to underwrite career development, the company would have to participate in nonrecording income. (Goodman, 2010, p. 257)

With revenue from the sale of recorded music shrinking, major labels therefore sought a return on their investment from other revenue streams.[5] The position of major labels—that it was *their* risk capital that built the platform upon which income could be generated from the other streams—was a convincing one. While many artists and their representatives initially resisted what they termed a 'rights grab' (see Morrow, 2006, p. 136), they clearly saw their best chance of building a sustainable career in signing a 360 deal 'if you want to sell a million "things"... the probabilities are in being with a global record company' (Goodman, 2010, p. 258). Around this time, the major labels' rosters became younger as established artists had less incentive to sign over additional rights.

Our research findings identified that a direct signing to a major label will now, most likely, involve a 360 deal. As Dean Ormston (Head of Member Services Group for collecting society APRA AMCOS) noted, 'I think that the opportunity for career artists is in understanding their rights and the potential for deriving income from each of their channels

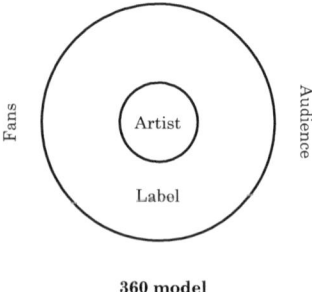

Fig. 2.1 360 model showing label intermediation between artists and audiences/fans

or revenue streams. Increasingly artists will need to be more sophisticated about how they manage or exploit each channel.' Likewise, Robert Scott (Founder of Source Music Publishing and Licensing and Creative Manager, Embassy Music Publishing and Music Sales) posited:

> I think that what's happening is the 360 is [sic] more of a swing to management, I think managers have never been as important as they are now. What are managers? They basically manage 360, so sometimes that management is in a label, or a publishing company or wherever it needs to be… I think that 360 deals are just par for the course and they have always existed and if anything they're not nearly as nasty as they once were back in the day. If you look at Elvis or even The Beatles, their early catalogue, their publishing rights were abandoned.

Scott is arguing here that 360 deals are not a new phenomenon. Instead he noted that they are, in some ways, reminiscent of the origins of the recording industry. This is because at the outset of this industry artists tended to assign all of their rights to one entity. Nevertheless, whether the 360 model (see Fig. 2.1) is considered to be old or new, it is clearly the dominant model within the new *recording* business of music.

The Entrepreneur Model (Model 2)

In contrast to the 360 model, the issue of risk capital is fundamental to understanding the recording industry's additional response to disruption. This response involved the externalisation of risk onto the artists themselves. Indeed, major labels are faced with a choice between 360 deals or a more streamlined approach. Australian artist manager Todd Wagstaff outlined this choice:

> Labels have a choice now—they can make up for that decline [in physical sales] with either reactionary 360 deals... or they can take the cost out of the part they do really well and then get out there and do that part with some 'risk free gusto'. (Wagstaff cited in Brandle, 2012)

The part(s) that major record labels arguably do well are marketing and distribution. A streamlined approach essentially involves labels becoming service providers to artists' businesses, meaning that artists pay for, create, and own all of their assets. This approach complicates arguments that artists can cut out intermediaries by working as self-managed entrepreneurs (see Collins & Young, 2010; Scott, 2012), because this model (see Fig. 2.2) enables artists to stay independent while working with, and through, major label marketing and distribution services. In the new music business environment, several of our participants noted that intermediaries were vital to artist viability and sustainability, particularly as careers developed.

As Fig. 2.2 shows, there are many different patterns of relationships between artists and intermediaries in the music industries. These patterns

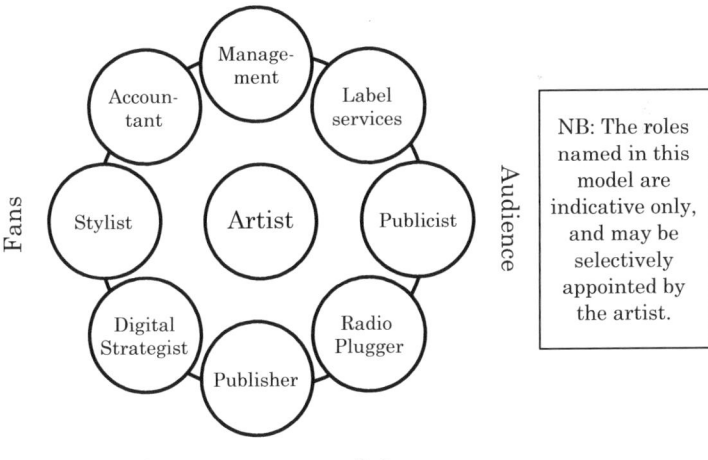

Entrepreneur model

Fig. 2.2 Entrepreneur model showing the network of potential personnel and roles across the new music industries

can evolve and devolve across an artist's career; they may also be different in various geographic territories. The complexity of the new music business therefore necessitates new ways of conceptualising career development. We do, however, acknowledge that an artist can release a minimum viable product[6] (MVP) (Robinson, 2001; Ries, 2011, p. 93) directly to fans (see also the DIY model). Nonetheless, for a sustainable career, artists often need to engage a number of intermediaries and the pattern of intermediary relationships formed should be subject to the developing needs of the artist's startup partnership or company.

The DIY Model (Model 3)

Prior to the digitisation of music, DIY self-management was most commonly associated with the 1980s punk phenomenon. Anderson (2012) noted that punk bands challenged the status quo within the music business, circumventing the recording, manufacturing, and marketing services of major record labels (p. 11). Such business practices were connected to an ideology of liberalism, which cast the artist as authentic (Wiseman-Trowse, 2008) and free from the demands of the mainstream marketplace. By seizing the means of production, punk musicians were therefore placed at the centre of meanings and values associated with the notion of authenticity. Gracyk noted:

> The unifying thread… is an assumption that the unique individual is basic to authenticity. In a word, liberalism: there is no essential, common good beyond whatever autonomous individuals seek and choose as most worthy for themselves. (Gracyk cited in Wiseman-Trowse, 2008, p. 42)

The perception that record labels and the industry used to restrict the artist's true self through an adherence to market fundamentalism is challenged by contemporary DIY artists. DIY artists, themselves operating within the new business of music, have assumed positions within the new music industries where they are directly concerned about the market (see Fig. 2.3). Anderson (2012) noted:

> In the Web Age, the DIY punk movement's co-opting of the means of production turned into regular people using desktop publishing, then websites, then blogs, and now social media. Indie-pressed vinyl became YouTube music videos. Four-track tape recorders became ProTools and iPad music apps. Garage bands became Apple's GarageBand. (p. 13)

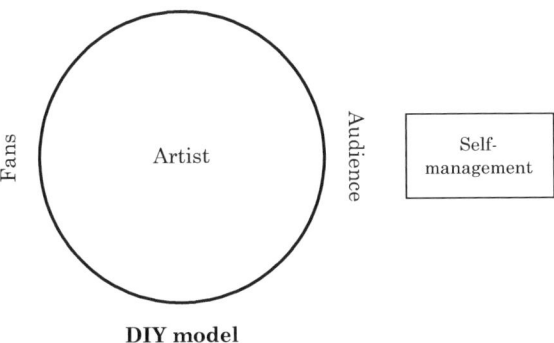

Fig. 2.3 DIY model, showing that the artist bears the sole responsibility

The ubiquity of personal media devices, such as the mobile phone, allows artists with sufficient creative self-efficacy (see Jaussi and Randel, 2014) to write and record their own music, and to release it through digital outlets. Goodman (2010) explained that 'the web had decimated CD sales, but it had also made it possible for anyone to post music online—and the result had been a flood of new and undifferentiated releases' (p. 258). This 'flood' of artist releases means that the DIY artist now needs to take responsibility for not only the creation of new creative material, but also for strategising how to stand out in a crowded marketplace (discussed further in Chapter 3).

Our research has shown that DIY approaches have become a necessary stage in all career development models, as research participant Dean Ormston noted:

> Without doubt YouTube provides a massive promotional platform for artists—but the economic return for the vast majority of artists is very small. The endless YouTube appetite for both commercial and User Generated Content has meant there's now a huge onus on the artist and content owners generally to monitor how and where their work is exploited.

Ormston continued, noting:

> While a DIY business model for artists sounds sexy on first glance, artists often comment on being inundated in managing the promotion and distribution of their work—'I am drowning in it. I am not actually doing what I wanted to do which is write songs and perform.' There's been a massive workload shift to the artist—in the past someone else would have been doing it for the artist.

A massive workload therefore lies with DIY artists because they have to manage their own presence through social media. One solution is for the artist to engage with the entrepreneur model and work with intermediaries. Vanessa Picken (Director of digital marketing agency Comes with Fries), posited that 'there is strength in the market, where independent artists are empowered via companies like Comes With Fries to deliver on their releases through a multitude of label services.' DIY artists can therefore transition to being entrepreneurs and appoint intermediaries to assist in career development. Before transitioning to entrepreneur, however, artists typically need to demonstrate some traction with an audience before they can attract the intermediaries.

A Question of Risk

A core question that emerged through our research was around risk, and how it is devolved in the new career models. While artists can now drive their own careers and/or build their own team, the financial risk essentially lies with the artists. The significance of the team in this approach was highlighted by Vanessa Picken:

> You really need to find the best team that enhances your work because if you're an independent artist you have all of the control to find that group. So, a lot of the work I do is helping people find their own independent team that replicates or replaces the old traditional label model.

Major labels can thus become more reactive by waiting to see which artists demonstrate signs of effective strategies and exponential growth before assisting in subsequent career development.

Major record labels devolving risk relates primarily to our Entrepreneur and DIY models, although in the digital economy, all three models may be relevant particularly if labels function as service providers. This may occur in instances whereby labels devolve the risks pertaining to record production to artists and, in some instances, to their managers. In this context, the label's traditional[7] power relationship to artists has changed as the artists take on more financial risk. With larger entities in the music business externalising financial risk by making asset generation and marketing spend the artist's responsibility, artists need to be educated regarding how to manage such risk.

As there is now 'an abundance of distribution outlets, and, as a result, a scarcity of audience attention' (Morrow, 2011, p. 106), smaller industry players are able to establish sustainable businesses in the new music industries. Participants discussed the ways in which 'the music industry' has changed with the emergence of smaller entities. However, our research also identified that there are now a number of large entities that generate revenue from the aggregate of the many smaller entities or artists. This emerged as an interesting juxtaposition of business types in the new industries. Noting the growth of some organisations, Robert Scott explained:

> Majors have never been bigger, look at Universal just taking over EMI… there's a major concentration happening with the labels as well as everywhere else. IMPALA have been arguing in Europe that this is really dangerous, because obviously they've got too much market share now. The last thing anyone would want is if they were to walk into iTunes and say, 'We won't give you our 65% of the market unless you give us this', a greater rate or a bigger percentage. Of course, this rivalry between indie and major is very quickly being overtaken by the power of the tech companies now. The music industry is fast becoming an Apple versus Amazon versus Spotify world.

The reciprocity between small and large business entities can also be examined through the example of artist management company, Parker + Mr French. According to its founder, Wagstaff (cited in Brandle, 2012), the company engineered a deal with Universal Music Australia (UMA) that enabled the artists it manages to stay independent *while* working with UMA. The concept was that the artists take on the risk of their own career development by investing *in* themselves. If successful, the artists then receive a greater return than they would if the label had advanced them money in a more traditional way under a 360 deal. A new entity alignment such as this falls within the Entrepreneur model (Fig. 2.2). Rather than the artist-entrepreneur being a force of disruptive 'creative destruction' (Schumpeter, 1939), there is potential for reciprocal revenue generation to emerge through this form of entrepreneurship. This business alignment suits entities that derive economic benefit from the aggregate of the many artists who are now able to access an audience, as Anderson (2006) noted:

> The democratized tools of production are leading to a huge increase in the numbers of producers. Hyperefficient digital economics are leading to new markets and marketplaces. And finally, the ability to tap the distributed intelligence of millions of consumers to match people with the stuff that suits them best is leading to the rise of all sorts of new recommendation and marketing methods, essentially serving as the new tastemakers. (p. 57)

By becoming more reactive aggregators, record labels potentially benefit from distributed intelligence amongst consumers within the marketplace(s) in which they operate.

Linear to Circular Career Development

Career development in the new music industries is a complex mix of creative practices, business acumen and maximising opportunities; it is a process centred on discovery of the artist by an audience/fans that has the potential to stimulate interest from and through a range of industries.[8] This represents a paradigm shift in career development and industry engagement and is represented below in the transition from the traditional linear model (see Fig. 2.4) to a circular model (see Fig. 2.5). Watson (2013)[9] described the traditional linear process as:

> The artist would find a manager, and the manager would have relationships with the record company and the booking agent… And those people would get you exposed through the venues, and through the media outlets and the audience would then shop from that menu.

Indeed, our research confirmed that career development is no longer dependent upon finding the right gatekeeper. With the notion of artists finding someone who will 'do it all for them' being passé, a contemporary way to conceptualise the process of career development involves a circular model, as Watson described:

> The artist is able to communicate directly with the fan, and then when the artist engages enough fans, all these other people go 'hey, there's something going on there, I think I can help grow that' and the journalist thinks that, the TV show thinks that, the promoter thinks that, and everybody starts to come on board. But instead of it going—artist—industry person—industry person—industry person—fan. It now actually goes—artist—fan—industry—artist. It's a circle that begins with that artist-fan communication.

As depicted in the circular model (see Fig. 2.5), artists can now have a direct relationship with fans in a range of contexts (such as via social media, blogs and through personalised artist generated fan emails).

The circular model sheds light on the paradox of the 'liberal artist' (Wiseman-Trowse, 2008, p. 42) in the digital age, and represents the

Fig. 2.4 Linear model showing traditional intermediation between artist and fans

relationships that many artists have with the larger entities such as major record labels. As noted above, a consequence of this is that record labels are able to become more *reactive*, effectively testing the market before choosing which product to support. In this context, 'bottom up' and 'top down' are not opposing concepts, but instead work together within the new business of music. As a consequence, both traditional and non-traditional elements function as new gatekeeping components of the industries.

The 'bottom up' paradigm refers to a certain type of web utopianism that stemmed from the Internet's (only partly realised) promise to connect artists directly to fans, a form of utopianism that has been previously discussed in terms of 'cutting out the intermediaries' (Collins & Young, 2010; Scott, 2012). Prior to this, the record label system dominated because the major companies had unrivalled control over, and access to, distribution, sales and marketing resources. In the new business of music, while access to the more typical methods of distribution, sales and marketing resources may still be contested, the controlling entities have morphed into new, yet familiar, versions of themselves. In some ways, though, this has seen a levelling of gatekeeping roles in the new music industries that lead to a 'flattened structure' (Hesmondhalgh & Meier, 2015) that is facil-

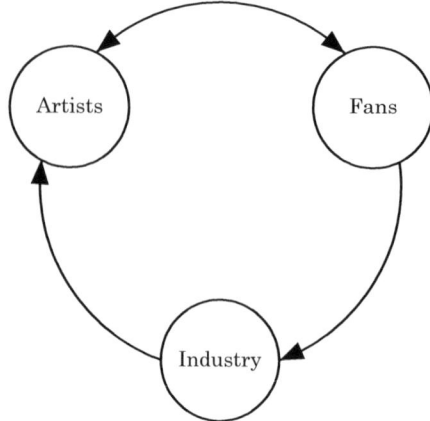

Fig. 2.5 Circular model encompassing artists, fans, and industry

itated by the new digital platforms and accessibility to a range of technologies. It complements the circular model outlined above by highlighting the changes in roles and associated functions. McGuigan (2010) argued, however, that the complex changes to the digital environment have not led to greater variety in terms of the content being produced because soft creativity is more often the end product which leads to 'a great deal of standardisation and uniformity' (p. 239).

With major labels being more reactive and many artists and their teams embracing standardisation, uniformity across products may be viewed as attempts to emulate other successful product/s and strategies. This concept was discussed by Marc Marot and Keith Harris during a panel discussion at the Vienna Music Business Research Days conference in Vienna in October 2014[10] (see also Morrow & Li, 2016). Our research findings suggested that there is a significant degree of soft creativity at the starting point of the circular system of the new music industries, as Damian Cunningham (Director of Audience and Sector Development, National Live Music Office) noted:

> In theory an artist can now produce a track at home in 30 minutes and in a further 15 minutes can effectively be selling the track on a global facing platform… The ability to do it more quickly means that there are a lot more people producing music, and when a lot more people are doing it, it can all look the same.

Cunningham noted that the speed at which artists can release material sometimes means that they do not allow themselves time to step back and think about how they can produce content that is more unique. Therefore, the speed of releases does not always enable artistic output to exemplify hard creativity. While Madden and Bloom (2001) note that 'soft creativity is perhaps the predominant form of artistic creativity' (p. 414), in the new music industries this softer form of creativity infers that there will be less chance of standing out in a crowded marketplace.

Conclusion

Each of the three career development models (360, Entrepreneur, and DIY) outlined in this chapter require artists to demonstrate exponential growth at the outset (that is, the circular process of career development). This is despite the issue that early growth does not always enable artists to establish sustainable careers in either the short or longer term. Within the new business of music, each of these career models features (or potentially features) more risk and responsibility being located with the artist. For this reason, our research identified the DIY artist as a significant, viable and fundamentally necessary model within the new music industries. It is relevant because it potentially leads to subsequent career models.

One way to conceptualise the patterns of relationships that artists may form with intermediaries in subsequent career models involves a bicycle wheel analogy (Watson, 2002). This analogy is relevant in describing the potential career-building process. It is important to note that we have chosen not to include the manager in the 'hub' or centre of the career-building process in either the 360 model or the Entrepreneur model even though we acknowledge that an artist manager is often typical and warranted. We do so for the following reasons: (1) the artist is free to undertake management responsibilities, (2) the artist in the new career models is likely to assume risk, and (3) a label may assume managerial roles and functions.

In each of our models, the career-building process (in whatever form or combination of roles is determined) remains pivotal, with more responsibility residing with the artist to coordinate and/or decide upon these roles. There are many different patterns of relationships between artists and intermediaries in the music industries, and the pattern of relationships formed is subject to the developing needs of the artist's startup partnership or company.

Notes

1. In this context, the word 'neoliberal' refers to the atomization of the music industries caused by the increased individualisation of the artist (particularly with regard to risk-taking). The argument here is that the record business has been subject to a shift from organised capitalism to neoliberal capitalism, and as a result more financial risk has been externalised onto the artist.
2. This chapter examines the extent to which there is still a great deal of standardisation and uniformity in terms of artistic content (see also McGuigan, 2010) in the new music industries. Artists themselves are now able to control the processes leading to such standardisation in many instances, rather than major record labels.
3. Exchange value refers to the quantitative aspect of value (for example, in this context, how much money is exchanged for recorded music); use value is the qualitative aspect of value (for example, in this context, the level of enjoyment someone gets from listening to music).
4. Such a critical engagement with the term 'music industry' has featured in numerous studies of the music business, such as in Morrow (2006) and more recently Tschmuck (2016).
5. According to Goodman (2010), the band Paramore was the first young band to sign an all-encompassing 360 deal with WMA, while he cites EMI's landmark 360 deal with Robbie Williams as the first to be agreed with an established artist (p. 255).
6. A Minimum Viable Product (MVP) is defined by Robinson (2001) and Ries (2011) as being a new product which is literally minimally viable. Rather than waiting to release a product to market when it is deemed to be more viable than minimally so, an MVP allows the person, or group of people, developing it 'to collect the maximum amount of validated learning about customers with the least effort'. (Ries, 2011, p. 93).
7. Our use of the term 'traditional' reflects the conventional, popular music industry. Participants typically noted this context as traditional.

8. While we focus on the new music industries, we also discuss some industries in this chapter that are not specifically related to music. We therefore acknowledge that some of the new industries are not dedicated music industries but encompass music practices such as crowdfunding sites.
9. All comments attributed to John Watson in this chapter are taken from a keynote question-and-answer session he delivered at the BIGSOUND conference in Brisbane on 12 September, 2013. BIGSOUND is an industry conference that includes presentations, panels and performance showcases (BIGSOUND, 2016).
10. This was the Fifth Vienna Music Business Research Days on the *Monetization of Music in the Digital Age*, held on 3 October, 2014, at the Institute for Cultural Management and Cultural Studies, Vienna, Austria.

References

Anderson, C. (2006). *The long tail*. New York: Hyperion.
Anderson, C. (2012). *Makers: The new industrial revolution*. New York: Crown Business.
Australian Recording Industry Association. (2014). *2013 ARIA wholesale figures*. Retrieved February 24, 2016, from http://www.aria.com.au/documents/MediaRelease-2013ARIAWholesaleFigures.pdf.
BIGSOUND. (2016). BIGSOUND. Retrieved February 2, 2016, from http://www.qmusic.com.au/bigsound/2015/index.cfm?contentID=860
Brandle, L. (2012). The hot seat: Todd Wagstaff, Parker + Mr. French. *The Music Network*. Retrieved February 24, 2016, from http://larsbrandle.com/the-hot-seat-todd-wagstaff-parker-mr-french
Collins, S., & Young, S. (2010). A view from the trenches of music 2.0. *Popular Music and Society, 33*(3), 339–355.
Goodman, F. (2010). *Fortune's fool: Edgar Bronfman Jr., Warner music, and an industry in crisis*. New York: Simon and Schuster.
Hesmondhalgh, D., & Meier, L. (2015). Popular music, independence and the concept of the alternative in contemporary capitalism. In J. Bennett & N. Strange (Eds.), *Media independence* (pp. 94–116). Abingdon, UK/New York: Routledge.
IFPI (International Federation of Phonographic Industry). (2011). *Recording industry in numbers 2011*. Retrieved June 5, 2011, from http://www.ifpi.org/recording-industry-in-numbers.php

IFPI (International Federation of Phonographic Industry). (2014). *Digital music report 2014*. Retrieved January 9, 2015, from http://www.ifpi.org/downloads/Digital-Music-Report-2014.pdf

IFPI (International Federation of Phonographic Industry). (2015). *Digital music report 2015*. Retrieved December 4, 2015, from http://www.ifpi.org/downloads/Digital-Music-Report-2015.pdf

Jaussi, K., & Randel, A. (2014). Where to look? Creative self-efficacy, knowledge retrieval, and incremental and radical creativity. *Creativity Research Journal, 26*(4), 400–410.

Leyshon, A., Webb, P., French, S., Thrift, N., & Crewe, L. (2005). On the production of the musical economy after the Internet. *Media Culture and Society, 27*(2), 177–209.

Madden, C., & Bloom, T. (2001). Advocating creativity. *International Journal of Cultural Policy, 7*(3), 409–436.

McGuigan, J. (2010). Creative labour, cultural work and individualisation. *International Journal of Cultural Policy, 16*(3), 323–335.

Morrow, G. (2006). *Managerial creativity: A study of artist management practices in the Australian popular music industry*. Unpublished PhD thesis, Macquarie University, Sydney, Australia.

Morrow, G. (2011). Sync agents and artist managers: A scarcity of attention and an abundance of onscreen attention. *Screen Sound, 2*, 104–117.

Morrow, G., & Li, F. (2016). China's music industries: Top down in the bottom up age. In P. Wikström & R. Defillippi (Eds.), *Business innovation and disruption in the music industry*. Cheltenham, UK: Edward Elgar Publishing.

Nordgård, D. (2016). Lessons from the world's most advanced market for streaming services. In P. Wikstrom & R. Defillippi (Eds.), *Business innovation and disruption in the music industry* (pp. 175–190). Cheltenham, UK: Edward Elgar Publishing.

Ries, E. (2011). *The lean startup*. New York: Crown Business.

Robinson, F. (2001). *A proven methodology to maximize return on risk*. Retrieved February 24, 2016, from http://www.syncdev.com/minimum-viable-product/

Schumpeter, J. (1939). *Business cycles: A theoretical, historical and statistical analysis of the capitalist process*. New York: McGraw Hill.

Scott, M. (2012). Cultural entrepreneurs, cultural entrepreneurship: Music producers mobilising and converting Bourdieu's alternative capitals. *Poetics, 40*, 237–255.

Tschmuck, P. (2016). From record selling to cultural entrepreneurship: The music economy in the digital paradigm. In P. Wikström & R. Defillippi (Eds.), *Business innovation and disruption in the music industry* (pp. 13–32). Cheltenham, UK: Edward Elgar Publishing.

Watson, J. (2002). What is a manager? In M. McMartin, S. Eliezer, & S. Quintrell (Eds.), *The music manager's manual*. Sydney, Australia: The Music Manager's Forum.

Watson, J. (2013). *Keynote Q & A with John Watson*. Interviewed by N. Megel on 12 September 2013, *BigSound*, The Judith Wright Centre, Brisbane, Australia.

Williamson, J., & Cloonan, M. (2007). Rethinking the music industry. *Popular Music, 26*(2), 305–322.

Wiseman-Trowse, N. (2008). *Performing class in British popular music*. Basingstoke, UK: Palgrave Macmillan.

CHAPTER 3

Standing Out in the Crowd

Abstract While the opportunities for accessing and sharing music are now extensive, this chapter addresses the ability to be noticed or heard. This can pose significant challenges for artists. An analysis of career development within the new music industries suggests that tension between creativity and management roles dissipates when the artist becomes an artist-entrepreneur or is DIY. These options, however, require artists to be strategic in their individuality and branding. The branding options extend to online presentation and access, as well as merchandising and image. This chapter discusses various artist strategies including startups, online direct-to-fan services, and intermediaries, focusing on hard creativities in these areas.

Keywords Startups • Direct-to-fan services • Intermediaries • Online

This chapter focuses on musical creativity by exploring the innovation, novelty and groundbreaking creativities present within the new music industries. It features artist strategies and online direct artist-to-fan services as examples of business creativity *as* invention, and, arguably, innovation.[1] Standing out in the new music industries necessitates artistic and business creativities. Within this context, this chapter examines whether an artist's career can be considered a startup. We argue that due to the ambiguity surrounding the term 'novel' in definitions of hard artistic creativity, some artists are operating in circumstances of extreme uncertainty. This is evident in attempts to create art *and* to stand out in a crowded marketplace. Uncertainty stems from the question of whether an audience will favourably receive a creative work, deem it to be novel and innovative, and help business models to succeed.

Our analysis of career development within the new music industries suggests that tension between creativity and management (Bilton, 2007) dissipates when the artist becomes self-managed (DIY model) or operates as an artist entrepreneur (Entrepreneur model). This ironically simplifies the notion of the 'liberal artist' (Wiseman-Trowse, 2008) and the discourses of authenticity associated with it. It also raises interesting questions regarding the suitable application of the lean startup methodology (Ries, 2011) to career development in the new music industries. The uncertainty and ambiguity surrounding the novelty of hard artistic creativities, and the question of who decides what is creative in the digital ecology, means that startup methodologies for addressing uncertainty in relation to both hard artistic creativity, and the business/es around it, are applicable.

This chapter also addresses questions of whether artists can 'pivot'[2] (Ries, 2011, p. 24) in similar ways to other startups. The new music business brings with it much countercultural baggage (see Goodman, 1997, p. 10), adding complications that do not apply to non-music startups; discourses of authenticity, nuanced branding signification, subcultural capital (Thornton, 2006) and coolness are at play in complex and rapidly evolving ways. How an artist is branded needs to be reflective of the music and of the individual/s involved, and is often genre-specific. This branding extends to online presentation and access, as well as traditional and non-traditional merchandising.

Artist Startups

We propose conceptualising artists' careers as startups, with particular attention to definitions and understandings of artistic creativity in the digital ecology. The circular model of career development means that, to varying degrees, artists are exposed to more financial risk in the new music industries and thus need to know how to manage this risk. We argue therefore that the notion of a minimum viable product (MVP) (Robinson, 2001; Ries, 2011, p. 93) is useful here for managing such risk. This notion can assist artists to discern market exploitation and market-building as two different stages of the processes of marketisation. Our research suggests that many artists spend large amounts of risk capital in their attempts to produce a fully developed product that they can release into the market in order to kick-start their career. For example, in considering attempts by Australian bands to gain an audience by attending and disseminating their product at leading international music festival and conference South by South West (SXSW) in Austin, Texas, USA, Tom Harris (Founder of White Sky Music, a specialist music business management and bookkeeping company) warned that Australian artists potentially 'waste' significant amounts of money because it is difficult to stand out in such a competitive environment. Such mismanagement of funds also happens because some artists wait until they have a fully developed product before they release it, and therefore confuse market exploitation with market-building. In this context, there is often no pre-existing market to exploit because it has not, as yet, been built. The risk capital required to prepare for potential markets is extensive and may incur little initial return.

Many definitions of startups exist in the literature (Jolly, 2003; Ries, 2011; Damodaran, 2011; Blank & Dorf, 2012; Graham, 2012; Eisenmann, Ries, & Dillard, 2012). Blank and Dorf (2012) argued that a startup is 'a temporary organization in search of a scalable, repeatable, profitable business model' (p. xvii). The word 'search' implies that a startup organisation is breaking new ground in an emerging/immature market, while the word 'temporary' alludes to the fact that startups either evolve into established businesses or cease to exist. These words are also used here to differentiate startups from new small businesses that are engaging in soft business creativities because they are using pre-existing business models and are not in a temporary phase that involves searching for a business model. Graham (2012) and Damodaran (2011) associate startups with growth, while Jolly (2003) discusses failure as being a necessary pre-condition of success in this area by noting that restarting is often part of the process.

Blank (2013) noted that because '75% of all startups fail' (p. 1), the lean startup methodology identified by Ries (2011) has become dominant in the startup field because it theoretically reduces risk. Blank (2013) stated that this method favours 'experimentation over elaborate planning, customer feedback over intuition, and iterative design over traditional 'big design up front' development' (p. 1). We focus on this approach because it potentially enables artists to test assumptions about their music, the organisational structures around their music, and their overall brand in ways that avoid the pitfalls of market-building/market exploitation confusion. It therefore limits their exposure to risk. The notion of an MVP (Robinson, 2001; Ries, 2011, p. 93) is key to this process. Compared with other startups, artists can easily release an MVP through social media in order to start the process of market building. Artists' careers can therefore be considered as startups because they meet Ries's definition of 'a human institution designed to create a new product or service under conditions of extreme uncertainty' (Ries, 2011, p. 27). Ries also argued that 'successful startups are full of activities associated with building an institution' (p. 28). According to Ries, institution-building activities include the securing and coordination of creative employees to facilitate a company culture that 'delivers results' (Ries, 2011, p. 28). Thus, a startup involves building a somewhat bureaucratic enterprise.

An artist's career in the new music industries is an enterprise. The DIY and Entrepreneur models (see Chapter 2) detail how the 'artist' extends beyond purely artistic endeavours. However, it is important to note that not all artists create a genuinely '*new product* or *service* under conditions of *extreme uncertainty*' (Ries, 2011, p. 27, author's emphasis). 'Innovation' is interesting here and is interchangeable with 'novelty' in the context of defining hard artistic creativity. Ries noted that the exact cloning of another business venture is not considered a startup because 'its success depends only on execution—so much so that this success can be modelled with high accuracy' (Ries, 2011, p. 29). Our argument therefore is that artists attempting to achieve *novelty* through their work by incorporating hard artistic creativity cannot model their success with high accuracy and may therefore be viewed as startups.

ARTISTIC CREATIVITY

Definitions of artistic creativity[3] are fundamental for conceptualising artists' careers as startups. Creativity is most often defined as the process of making useful, novel products (Csikszentmihalyi, 1996; Mumford, 2003; Kilgour, 2006; Weisberg, 2006, 2010). In addition to this, Madden and Bloom (2001) outline the issues involved in the process of valuing artistically 'hard' and 'soft' creative outcomes (see Chapter 1). They expand on this notion by questioning the direct application of invention–cognition definitions of creativity in the arts sphere because such an application implies that 'artistic creativity is about generating new artistic ideas' (Madden & Bloom, 2004, p. 135) whereas it also typically involves aspects of tradition and affect.

The ideas here highlight the ambiguity surrounding novelty within the new music industries. In addition, the concept of creativity within social systems (Csikszentmihalyi, 1996) fuels this ambiguity. Negus and Pickering (2000) also argued that 'creativity is a socio-culturally constructed concept that requires value judgements by others in order to acknowledge creative outcomes' (p. 264). In the context of the new music industries, the question of who decides what is novel and creative is now dependent on a social system that has been broadened from music critics and the artist and repertoire (A&R) staff who work at record labels. Primarily through social media and online strategies, fans largely now determine at the outset of an artist's startup whether the music is novel and/or creative. The circular process of career development in the new music industries accentuates this, with social media, for example, crowdsourcing value judgements concerning creativity. The social media economy of shares and likes subsequently expands the size of the 'field' (Becker, 1982; Bourdieu, 1986; Csikszentmihalyi, 1996) of experts who decide the novelty of an artist's music and overall brand identity. Traditional intermediaries who constitute the field of popular music (such as artist managers and record label A&R representatives) are also reliant on the broader 'crowd' to provide quantitative metrics and data. This data can then be used to assess the potential exponential growth of an artist's career, and to determine whether to sign or not sign an artist.

Hard creativity in the digital environment is a socio-culturally constructed and located complex concept. Creating valued products increasingly hinges on the involvement of fans, which itself is dependent on creating novelty according to definitions of hard artistic creativity. As Le, Masse and Paris (2013) noted:

> Compared to traditional industries, where objectives are set and predefined by rationale targets or other activities such as fundamental scientific research, the cultural and creative industries present a more open-ended setting. (p. 57)

This open-ended setting, where value judgements are crowdsourced via social media, results in continuous uncertainty for artists attempting to generate the novelty required to achieve hard creativities. Furthermore, definitions of career success are likewise more open-ended in the new music industries (Hughes, Keith, Morrow, Evans, & Crowdy, 2013; Smith, 2013).

For original-music-producing artists, there is ambiguity surrounding the *novelty* they can generate through their hard artistic creativity. How or whether these trajectories can be defined as being successful attest to conditions of extreme uncertainty. In defining success for an artist's career, Joel Connolly (artist manager) noted:

> It depends on what [the band] want to achieve so we sit down with the band at the beginning and ask them what they want to achieve... We manage artists who want it to be their career and want to make money and have a career and who want it to be their job. Otherwise there is no point. We can't make money if they can't make money. For us, all of our artists are interested in earning a living from [music].

Artists' career development can meet the latter part of Ries's (2011) definition of a startup in two ways. First, the ambiguity surrounding the novelty they generate through their hard artistic creativity subjects them to extreme uncertainty. Second, the state of flux in the new music industries subjects startups to uncertainty in terms of career development opportunities. In this context, career development increasingly requires an innovative approach to be noticed in a crowded marketplace.

Developing a Brand

Standing out in the new music industries involves novel creative developments in both artistic and business endeavours. It involves the organisational structure surrounding the artist, and also the various forms of musical and visual media they produce (for example, music videos, gig posters, album art, set designs, merchandise designs and social media). Artists may be able to 'pivot' (Ries, 2011, p. 24) their product in ways similar to those used in non-music startups. The need to generate novelty is constant, and to create novelty artists must carefully position and construct their identity and branding. Watson noted:

> [Artists] have to plan to be constantly remarkable. Not just on day one, but on day ten, twenty, one hundred, and all the way through the life cycle of the project. And the life cycle of the product will be shorter. (Watson, 2013)[4]

This constant necessity for innovation needs to be balanced with a consistent artist identity or brand. The brand of an artist is essential in strategizing their career and in developing capital among audiences and other stakeholders. The theory concerning cultural, social and economic capital (Bourdieu, 1986) is useful here in highlighting the various forms of capital at play. Morrow (2006) links cultural capital with the notion of a brand in a discussion of artist management practices in the music industries, noting that a brand 'is the qualitative or cultural experience of the product' (p. 54); effective branding builds social and cultural capital (Morrow, 2006, p. 57). The notion of subcultural capital (Thornton, 2006) is crucial to the concept of standing out, as it directly relates to constructs of *authenticity*[5] and *coolness*, which form a core element of the marketing process within the new music industries. Other kinds of capital are also relevant; for example, social capital today is quantified through social media data, in terms of fan numbers and interaction.

Artists therefore need to decide to link their music, their identity, their social structure and the lifestyle that their brand represents. Liz Tripodi (vocal teacher, entrepreneur, and performer) summarised this by noting that 'the artist needs to think of themselves as a brand'. Joel Connolly (artist manager) likewise noted that artists can be reluctant to brand themselves:

> Artists rarely think about [the brand]. They think about their 'image' as they call it—'We don't want people to see us this way.' I think it has always been important. It's just easier to see now.

These considerations raise questions as to the overall development of brands. Leanne de Souza (artist manager) commented that an artist's branding process begins 'when they get their first Facebook page at 12'. This suggests that in the age of social media, some artists are, or need to be, cognisant of their personal brand from a very early stage in their artistic development. This has implications for parents who may be overseeing the artistic development of their children and the dissemination of product including YouTube clips. Visual design and strategies within the new music industries are therefore vital, especially given the visually focused nature of social media platforms such as YouTube, Instagram, Twitter, and Facebook. Long before the advent of social media, Negus (1992) astutely noted the relevance of visual marketing that 'involves an attempt to articulate the authenticity and uniqueness of an artist and to communicate this through a concise image which operates as a metonym for an act's entire identity and music' (p. 72).

Cumulatively, an artist's brand is amorphous, temporal and subject to development and change; it has symbolic value through its inherent meaning and how it is communicated (Ots & Hartmann, 2015, pp. 217–218). It is important for an artist's brand to be, at times, rejuvenated because what it means and communicates may change over time. An artist's brand may also be generated by its association with a patchwork of other brands that are fused together as part of an overall identity. This typically occurs when the artist works with a song publisher or synchronisation (sync) agent(s) in order to realise further opportunities (see Morrow, 2011). Interestingly, Matt Amery (artist) noted that for him the process of brand generation or regeneration occurred through the process of generating income:

> For us, a lot of our income comes from syncs and proportionately to what people have bought… it's so much more weighed to publishing and getting sync and ads and branding. That's where more of the money comes from so that's what we're looking for… Not so much focusing on people buying the music and the merch[andise].

Artists' brands are also created through written text. Artists, therefore, may also need to consider how publishing and/or a publicist may aid the construction/reconstruction of their brand. Stephen Green (publicist) noted that experienced publicists 'have spent 10, 15, whatever years absolutely nailing the idea of the psychology of media'. Publicists play a role in communicating understandings of music and the creative, and often youth-oriented, subculture/scenes surrounding it. This youth focus does, however, pose a challenge for career support and longevity, as Green further noted:

> triple j[6] is a network aimed at 18–24 year olds, how does a 35 year old songwriter, how are their songs, that they're writing today when they're 35, how do they relate to a 19 year old?

The Significance of Originality and Product

Despite the perception that many sectors of the music industries are youth-focused, the complexity of and opportunities afforded by the new music industries are such that artistic novelty may be recognised at any career stage. For example, Gotye (Wouter 'Wally' De Backer)—a Belgian-Australian, multi-instrumental musician and singer-songwriter—has developed his brand under the name 'Gotye'. This alias was derived from 'Gauthier', the French equivalent of 'Walter' or 'Wouter' (Pareles, 2011).

Initially, Gotye fronted a rock band (Downstares) and after it disbanded, he co-formed (in 2002 with Kris Schroeder) the Melbourne-based indie-pop trio The Basics (Alberts, 2016). He also released the first Gotye electronic music album, *Boardface* (Creative Vibes, 2003; Ankeny, 2016). After the success of his independently released second album *Like Drawing Blood* (Independent/Creative Vibes, 2006), Gotye was able to establish a permanent home in Melbourne's Southeast (Gotye.com, 2016). In 2010, he set up a recording studio in a barn at his parents' farm and set about recording tracks for his third album *Making Mirrors* (Gotye.com, 2016) which was released through Eleven and Universal Republic Records, and so traversed a combination of record labels.

In 2011, Gotye released the song 'Somebody That I Used to Know' (written by De Backer) featuring the New Zealand artist Kimbra. It was released as a single on 6 July 2011 and debuted at number 27 on the Australian Recording Industry Association (ARIA) Top 50 Singles Chart (Top40-Charts.com, n.d.). The song was boosted by endorsements from Ashton Kutcher and Lily Allen via Twitter (Twitter.com, 2011), exposing Gotye's music to their millions of followers (Jolly, 2011a, 2011b). 'Somebody That I Used To Know' peaked at number one in 18 countries and has been the number one single on iTunes in 46 countries (ABC, 2013). In 2012, it was a breakthrough song and reached number one on the Billboard Hot 100 (Billboard.com, 2012). This made Gotye the fifth Australian-based artist to do so and the second Belgian (after The Singing Nun in 1963) (Billboard.com, 2012). Gotye won five Australian Recording Industry Association (ARIA) Awards and received a nomination for an MTV EMA for Best Asia and Pacific Act (ABC, 2013). In 2013, Gotye won three Grammy Awards for Record of the Year, Best Pop Duo/Group Performance and Best Alternative Music Album (ABC, 2013).

'Somebody That I Used to Know' is an example of hard creativity because it is novel in its composition and production (see also Adams, 2014); hard creativity is also evident in the related film clip released in 2011 on YouTube and Vimeo. Directed by Natasha Pincus, the video has now been viewed over 758 million times (as of April, 2016). The video was listed at number 15 of the most-viewed videos on YouTube (as at April, 2013) (YouTube, 2013a) and the number 4 most-liked video of all time (YouTube, 2013b).

The Gotye example shows that an artist startup needs to feature a holistic MVP that involves music video, visual design, live performance and set designs, merchandise designs and online strategies. This multi-dimensional presence is the primary reason why artist startups typically require more input from intermediaries, not less; time, effort and skill are required to generate novelty in all of these areas. Additionally, artists now need to connect with many more distribution channels in order to make a number of impressions comparable to what would have occurred during the broadcast era (had the artist been fortunate enough to access a mainstream distribution outlet). As Watson (2013) noted:

> When I worked at Sony our boss had this great line: 'I loved the 70s, it was Countdown, then 2SM, then lunch.' He was half joking but he was also making a serious point. In those days if you covered that TV show and that radio station then that basically reached everybody. To reach the same percentage of the population nowadays you would probably have to do 100 different things because the audience is fragmented across all sorts of media. That's not a bad thing because instead of there being one or two powerful gatekeepers, there are now 100 different people who can make a difference and they're usually watching their audience and reacting to what they like rather than imposing their tastes on everyone else. Even so, it's now a lot more work to simultaneously get something into 100 channels—it would have been much easier to visit Countdown and 2SM and then go to lunch.

In order to better understand this new reality, a reconceptualization of the relationship between artist startups and various intermediaries is needed.

STARTUPS, ONLINE SERVICES AND VALIDATION

Many artist startups are faced with income insecurity (Throsby & Zednik, 2011) which appears to be exacerbated when artists experience difficulties in operating their business. The tension between creativity and business acumen endures even in education (see Bridgstock, 2012, p. 123), as the arts are arguably associated with a certain bohemian idealism. In this context, business acumen and artistic management are often framed as dull and bureaucratic concerns. Conversely, the more appealing term 'artist-entrepreneurship', as opposed to 'self-management', connotes something that is 'cool, innovative, and exciting' (Ries, 2011, p. 3).

Ries's (2011) lean startup methodology is useful as it helps to guide artist management strategies (whether through the process of self-management or through the service provision provided by a separate manager). Describing his methodology for 'hypothesis-driven entrepreneurship' (Eisenmann et al., 2012), Ries notes that 'the business and marketing functions of a startup should be considered as important as engineering and product development and therefore deserve an equally rigorous methodology to guide them' (p. 5). The methodology developed by Ries involves the process of validated learning. Validated learning (or validation) is a process that relies on the Build–Measure–Learn feedback loop (Ries, 2011, p. 228) afforded by launching an initiative/product, measuring its resultant efficacy and then using the data to inform subsequent development. Social media is one way through which the process of validation can occur. Its effectiveness can be substantiated by empirical data collected from fans and is 'a rigorous method for demonstrating progress' (Ries, 2011, p. 38). The direct artist-to-fan relationship enabled by social media can help artists address 'the extreme uncertainty' (Ries, 2011, p. 38) caused by the ambiguity surrounding the novelty they generate through hard creative endeavours. Discussing the complexity behind direct artist-to-fan communication, Matt Amery (artist) noted the level of integrity involved:

> It is more about what you stand for, which doesn't always come through your music, it might come through what you say online. People are more interested in, they might hear about your music, but then what hooks them is finding out about who you are.

This process of direct artist-to-fan communication is relevant not only for 'hooking' fans into being interested in the artist's work, but also 'hooking' intermediaries into being involved. Damian Cunningham[7] (Director of Audience and Sector Development, National Live Music Office) noted that for both emerging and high-profile artists developing an online presence is key:

> I think that is led by visual and easy online presences where people from a digital point of view are spreading the word rather than just going 'I really love that track, did you hear it on the radio?' It's like, 'Here's a 30 second grab on social media.'

Watson (2013) also discussed a growth in Facebook friends as a 'constant process of regular rewards'. This is another example of validation via social media. The iterative process of validated learning can encompass music, design, branding and other para-musical areas in a broad sense. As previously discussed, the circular communication cycle between artist–fan–industries–artist–fan–industries is only partly musical.

A number of online services have arisen to assist artists in direct-to-fan sales and marketing, in areas including ticketing, physical merchandise, web presence and digital merchandise (i.e. song downloads), as well as more specialised areas such as crowdfunding, gig booking, and email marketing. One of the earliest services, CDBaby, was founded in 1998 as a service enabling independent musicians to sell CDs of their work (Thompson, 1998). The service later expanded into digital distribution, offering artists the option of selling music digitally via services such as Apple iTunes (Thompson, 1998). CDBaby still exists today, but has adapted by diversifying into a number of other areas, including 'YouTube monetization, sync licensing, publishing royalty collection, and direct-to-fan tools for your website and Facebook' (CDBaby.com, 2016), as well as website creation (via its subsidiary company HostBaby), vinyl production, distribution of physical CDs to bricks-and-mortar stores (through partnership with Alliance Entertainment), merchandise production (via subsidiary company Merch.ly) and audio mastering (through partnership with Landr.com) (CDBaby.com, 2016). The proliferation of distinct services, from which artists can pick and choose according to their own unique requirements, shows the fragmentation of audiences across different media, and the need to engage in validated learning in order to develop a viable and sustainable career.

Other notable entities include Bandcamp, PledgeMusic, Topspin, Songkick, SonicBids, and Music Glue. Like CDBaby, many of these entities offer several services but are often associated with a primary service. For example, Bandcamp offers free downloads in exchange for the user's e-mail address, allowing the artist to build a database of fan e-mail addresses; it also allows artists to sell music downloads at any price point, including 'pay what you want' or minimum price. This approach empowers artists to manage their own fanbase data and also to decide how to monetise their work. Meanwhile, although Topspin offers a range of services including physical merchandise, downloads and ticketing, it is primarily associated with physical merchandise. In a *New York Times* profile of Topspin, Sisario (2011) noted that:

> it has developed a specialty of bundling physical goods with downloads. The company encourages bands to give songs away, wagering that curious fans will come back to buy more lucrative products like T-shirts or deluxe editions that can be combined at various price levels. The company's sales data seem to support that philosophy. Even with plenty of $2 videos and

$10 posters for sale, the average transaction on Topspin brings in $26; when tickets are involved, the average is $88. (Sisario, 2011)

The diversity of services available to artists in today's marketplace can be confusing for artists or managers who need to choose which ones best suit individual needs. However, as Brenden Mulligan (former strategic development vice-president at Sonicbids, an online booking service) noted, the proliferation of these services allows artists to employ those that best suit their fans, brand and engagement style, rather than 'one service that tries to be everything for everyone' (Mulligan, 2010).

With offices in London, New York and Sydney (Music Glue, 2016), Music Glue is an example of a digital marketing 'solution' that offers e-commerce tools for 'artists [and managers], venues, promoters and labels' (Music Glue, 2016). It provides the tools to 'empower... users to take control, own their data and sell anything, to anyone, anywhere, in any currency, in any language and via any device' (Music Glue, 2015). Music Glue's business model involves enabling artists, managers, promoters, venues, festivals and other participants in the music industries to set up a free online profile (Music Glue, n.d.). Each artist profile has 'a unique URL', is 'customisable' (with options for individualised branding) and is media/device-compatible (Music Glue, n.d.). In return for its services, Music Glue takes a 10% commission on sales (Music Glue, 2015). This includes ticketing, merchandise and digital sales (Music Glue, n.d.). In this way, Music Glue generates revenue only when the users of their service do (Music Glue, n.d.):

> Originally founded in 2007 by artists for artists, Music Glue is the only DIY platform that facilitates ticketing, chart eligible record sales, merchandise, fulfilment, crowdfunding, bundles and even more, in one simple to use package. Ultimately, we have created an artist-centric solution for the new global music industry that ensures more money goes back into the pockets of the music creators. (Music Glue, n.d.)

Through Music Glue's services, artists retain ownership of their fan data (Music Glue, 2015) which can be used to inform live performance and touring. Music Glue's service uses 'Google analytics to track visits' (Music Glue, n.d.) to the artists' profiles, thereby recording the geographical location of fans, which provides insight to potential touring destinations because artists can 'know where your fans are; what they buy' (Music Glue, n.d.). The founder of Music Glue, Mark Meharry (cited in Robinson, 2009) described the benefits of determining the location(s) of an artist fanbase:

> Enter Shikari are a great example. We have a global map set up where you can see all of your fans, you can drill down into particular towns. And for their booking agent, that's absolutely bang on for what they need to put their tours on around the world. And this year they'll be out on the road across the globe—based on where their fans are.

Once tour destinations are finalised, the artist (and/or manager/promoter) is able to approach venues/ticketing companies for an allocation of tickets, which is then sold directly to all fans. This cuts out secondary ticketing (and sales), a concern expressed by Mumford & Sons (see Lindvall, 2012; Mumford & Sons, 2015a) who are now a Music Glue user. Meharry (cited in West, 2015) explained the concept behind Music Glue's direct to fan ticketing and sales:

> By using Music Glue, artists have the greatest reach into the market and are now able to leverage that reach with retail. Yes, we eliminate secondary ticketing, however the biggest reasons to insist on large ticket allocations from promoters are data capture and upselling of products that the artist will make money from. (Meharry cited in West, 2015)

Using Music Glue's ticketing option, the artist (rather than the venue/ticketing company) is able to collect consumers' data. Music Glue therefore addresses the potential conflict of interests between the artist and the venue and/or ticketing company: an artist typically wants to retain the fan data to sell tickets to their future shows and to advertise the release of future recordings and other products, whereas the venue and/or ticketing company want to retain this data to upsell tickets to other artists' shows or other types of events. Meharry (cited in LeBlanc, 2015) noted the relevance of this function to the artist:

> [Artists] have enormous reach in the market now through all of the social media channels. They can reach a global marketplace, and what that marketplace is interested in is connecting with the artist directly. Our very original model was using an artist's music to locate its fans, and building up a database by exchanging music for data, for email addresses and locations. (Meharry cited in LeBlanc, 2015)

Music Glue users include high-profile artists such as Public Service Broadcasting, Mumford & Sons, Brian Ferry, Billy Bragg, Enter Shikari, and Boy & Bear (West, 2015).

A provider such as Music Glue affords an opportunity to validate learning through investigating options and testing those options. Such experimentation of business practices may be regarded as hypothesis-driven entrepreneurship. Ries (2011) explained that this concept 'begins with a clear hypothesis that makes predictions about what is supposed to happen. It then tests those predictions empirically' (Ries, 2011, pp. 56–57). Rather than thinking in reductionist ways that involve either an artist signing to a major label (potentially the 360 model) as the ultimate goal, or cutting out all intermediaries (as per the DIY model), artist and band startups need to develop more-nuanced hypotheses that can be tested through various experiments. Damian Cunningham articulated how services such as Music Glue, Bandcamp and Topspin Media can facilitate hypothesis-driven entrepreneurship. Cunningham posited that the processes and services offered by Music Glue do not 'seem to have boundaries' allowing artists to be 'as creative as what you want... you want to do a creative event, you want to do a merch sale, whatever you decide, those tools are flexible enough to work around it'. Therefore, the services provided by Music Glue have added a degree of flexibility when it comes to career-related hypothesis generation and experimentation.

In terms of the flexibility of entrepreneurial processes, Joe Vesayaporn (global sales director of Music Glue) provided the example of Enter Shikari as a band that has completed successful experiments in relation to ticket and merchandise sales. Enter Shikari control their own website (entershikari.com) and drive all traffic to this website (rather than to a ticketing service per se). In order to manage this process, Vesayaporn noted that Enter Shikari 'sent someone on the road with [their] shows to manage fans and scan tickets. They really took ownership and managed their ticket allocations at the venues they were playing'. Having educated their fans to purchase concert tickets directly from their website, Enter Shikari set up their own merchandise fulfilment company with their merchandise being sold directly via their website. In terms of this merchandising service, Vesayaporn noted that Music Glue 'are now offering that [option] out to other acts because they have done it right for themselves.' Through this process of learning how to do 'do it right for themselves', artists can gather reliable data that can be used to substantiate claims regarding current commercial success and the potential of future commercial success, as Cunningham noted: 'At any point you can give the equivalent of your fan profit and loss sheet and it is reliable hard data. I think that has changed things dramatically'. However, in terms of such experimentation, Cunningham also argued that 'sometimes "wrong" business decisions are the right things to do because of the creative outlet'. Vesayaporn cited other examples of bands such as Ben Howard and Mumford & Sons that began experimenting with direct artist-to-fan relations by using Music Glue's services. He noted that these bands have since been able to scale up their experiments as they have passed through the startup phase to become financially successful businesses. For instance, although the British band Mumford & Sons are signed to a mixture of independent and major labels such as Universal Music Group's Island imprint for the UK and Europe, to the large independent label Glassnote Records in North America and to Universal Music Australia's Dew Process imprint for Australia and New Zealand (Mumford & Sons, 2016), Vesayaporn recalled that:

> [Before they signed] record deals they were selling direct on the ticketing side of things… and from the very early days they were just putting stuff out via their Myspace or their website or via Music Glue, selling direct to fans, and they have continued to do that as they have grown.

Vesayaporn argued that this strategy provided them leverage to agree split territories deals across labels (as opposed to signing for the world with a major label out of a home territory).

Conceptualising Brand and Career Development

Mumford & Sons have long graduated the startup phase of their development and now offer direct-to-fan solutions. They sell tickets and merchandise directly to their fans (Mumford & Sons, 2016) and are noted for other entrepreneurial strategies. Vesayaporn, for example, noted that even though Mumford & Sons can draw the audience needed to play arena venues, they have conceptually elaborated on this by converting their arena shows into their own festival, which they headline (Mumford & Sons, 2015b). Mumford & Sons now sell tickets for their own Gentlemen of the Road and Stopover festivals directly to fans, as Vesayaporn explained:

> [This] is what they have done in the US and Canada and did in the UK in July where they promoted their own festival and sold 100 % of the tickets themselves. Again, they were doing that 4 years ago on a smaller scale. I

would say what they learned via direct-to-fan, and from management and themselves on ticketing, gave them confidence as they got bigger to do what they do.

Mumford & Sons' close control of their brand is to a large extent made possible through their touring and ticketing strategies. Fans have been 'educated' to purchase tickets via www.mumfordandsons.com, enabling the band to pursue some innovative live performance strategies. By using Music Glue as one of the primary ticketing outlets for their one-day festival in London in July 2013—which they claim 60,000 people attended (NME, 2013)—according to Vesayaporn, Mumford & Sons retained much of their fan data for future use. This meant that, in addition to controlling their own brand of Mumford & Sons, they also own the brand name of the festivals they headline around the world including the Gentlemen of the Road Stopover sub-brand.[8]

The examples above suggest that a useful way to conceptualise career development in the new music industries is to acknowledge that bands can release an MVP (Ries, 2011, p. 93) directly to fans, although to build a sustainable business they often need to engage a number of intermediaries. Determining which intermediaries they employ should be subject to the results of experiments that test various assumptions about the developing needs of their startup. In the specific case of Mumford & Sons, it is evident that Entrepreneur and DIY career models are traversed. However, these models are not used by Mumford & Sons as either/or options. Rather, they are used in unique combinations in a longitudinal sense and in terms of geographic territory.

The Melbourne artist Matt Walters (2015) has traversed career models and has launched an online platform for facilitating house concerts (parlour gigs) that is set to 'transform the live music economy' (Walters, 2015). Walters explained:

> From being signed to a major label, to touring with some incredible international artists, I've certainly experienced all the ups and downs the music business has to offer… Of course, with the traditional music model well and truly behind us, there is more emphasis than ever on playing live… This is what Parlour is all about. We are building a platform that will finally connect artists and hosts. (Walters, 2015)

The examples above illustrate how career development within the new industries has shifted from being linear to circular, and also demonstrate how the different career models outlined in Chapter 2 are mobilised in a way that is unique to each artist.

Central to career development in the new industries is the way artists engage with fans. Direct-to-fan strategies enable artists and artist startups to collect and retain fan data, instead of the data being collected by the venue(s) or third-party ticketing outlets. This data plays a crucial role in the validated learning that is important for an artist or an artist startup's ultimate success. As Vesayaporn argued, fan data is a means through which artists and artist startups can test their hypotheses by asking themselves such questions as:

> Do we have a range of T-shirts when it is actually signed vinyl and cool posters that sell? Or do we have a range of $40 posters that no one gives a shit about because they just want to get a nice T-shirt?

Through the use of fan data, artist startups can become adaptive organisations that automatically adjust their processes and performance to suit current conditions (Ries, 2011, p. 227). By collecting fan data at the outset, the artist startup's validated learning process that involves the Build–Measure–Learn feedback loop (Ries, 2011, p. 228) can become a continuous process. Through a service such as Music Glue, artists can work through a process of continuous iteration to develop their product(s). In this context, for an artist to be 'dropped'[9] by a label need not be a career setback.

Disruption and Resistance

The music industries are constituted by a complex web of intermediaries (Williamson & Cloonan, 2007, p. 305) and some benefit from the entrepreneurial efforts of artist startups, while others do not. In the live music industry, promoters and booking agents typically generate income on aggregate by working with a large number of artists. Conversely, artist and band startups (and artist managers) are more reliant on the revenue their startup and subsequent ongoing concerns generate. By enabling artists and artist startups to sell tickets directly to consumers, online direct-to-fan services may exacerbate tensions between artists who are attempting to stand out in the crowded marketplace and the artist managers, live promoters, and booking agents who would traditionally undertake or oversee the implementation of strategies to engage with audiences. Vesayaporn alluded to this when he stated that there is 'potential push back from all of the traditional players in their respective bits of the industry'. This disruptive nature is also highlighted in the following quote from company founder Mark Meharry regarding the silent backers behind Music Glue:

> We have high net worth shareholders. They would prefer not to be mentioned. They have nothing to do with the music industry, and are silent in the day-to-day operation. They love the idea of extreme disruption. (Meharry cited in LeBlanc, 2015)

The disruption afforded by direct-to-fan strategies may also be of benefit to a major or independent record label if it has a 360 deal with an artist. This is because these entities may benefit from the artist selling tickets directly because their respective commission of the band's live income does not first have the promoter's fee deducted from it. The tension caused by such disruption may not be attributed solely to the disintermediation that the Internet affords; the tension between artists (who are sometimes in partnership with record labels) and live music promoters and agents may also be fed by historical 'injustice'. Australian promoter Michael Chugg (2010), claimed that some artists were treated unfairly by agents:

> In the days before Dirty Pool came along and changed the system, you could do a deal with the club owner or the promoter to sell your act to them for $1500 and then tell your act they were getting $1200. (206)

Online ticketing services, such as those provided through Music Glue, therefore enable artists (and managers) to control (at least some of) the ticketing process and avoid the above scenario. Similarly, there are no opportunities for third-party kickbacks as artists are paid commensurate to their drawing power.

Conclusion

The growing complexity of the 'new' business of music (see Chapter 2) has led to an increased portfolio of responsibilities for artists. The shift from a scarcity of distribution outlets for music to an abundance of outlets in the digital music economy has made it vital to attract and retain an audience's attention by standing out in a crowded marketplace. Adding to the complexity of standing out is the evolution of social media which has expanded the field of experts who ultimately decide whether a particular artist's music and overall brand image is novel/creative: fans are therefore now a much more integral part of the field of music. In this context, artistic music products do not fit traditional product development models. They are subject to extreme uncertainty, and can be considered within the startup framework. However, artist startups are subject to additional layers of complexity when compared with other startups. These complexities include various discourses of artistic integrity, nuanced branding signification and the politics of subcultural capital/coolness, as well as the notion that artistic creativity involves invention and cognition *as well as* tradition and affect. Our research suggests that artists can 'pivot' (Ries, 2011, p. 24) like other startups, using entrepreneurial skill to lessen the tension between creativity and management that is sometimes associated with 'selling out'. This simplifies the notion of the liberal artist, and the discourses of authenticity associated with it. The lean startup methodology is applicable for managing the risk associated with career development in the new music industries; risk that is increasingly being placed on the shoulders of artists as they attempt to stand out in a crowded marketplace and attract various intermediaries through the circular career development process.

Notes

1. Madden and Bloom (2001) note that 'In the Schumpeterian distinction an invention is new, an innovation is both new and useful' (p. 419).
2. A 'pivot' involves a startup institution changing strategic direction, usually because a particular approach is not working. Ries (2011) notes that while products change constantly through the process of optimisation, a pivot is comparatively rare and even after a pivot the overarching vision rarely changes (149).
3. The term 'creativity' (in the singular) is deliberate in this section. Its use does not negate the existence of multiple artistic 'creativities' (Burnard, 2012). It is used here to broadly denote the concept rather than the more specific types of creative processes or musical creativities that are discussed in the opening paragraphs of this chapter and in Chapter 6.

4. All comments attributed to John Watson are taken from a keynote question and answer session he gave at BIGSOUND conference in Brisbane on 12 September 2013.
5. For more on authenticity see Chapter 4.
6. triple j is a taxpayer-funded, youth-oriented radio station on the FM band in Australia that broadcasts nationally. It forms part of the Australian Broadcasting Corporation (ABC) and it is one of the most important taste-making outlets for popular music in the country, with its influence extending to the sponsorship of festivals, online music outlets and competitions such as 'triple j unearthed', and the influential annual 'triple j Hottest 100' listener poll.
7. At the time of our interview in 2013, Cunningham was helping to launch Music Glue (an online direct artist-to-fan facilitator) in Australia.
8. Stopovers are festivals headlined by Mumford & Sons that focus on local communities.
9. The term 'dropped by a record label' can be somewhat misleading. It usually means that contractually the record label has committed to funding, releasing and promoting one album 'firm', and then they have a number of options for subsequent albums that *they* can decide to pick up or not. Therefore being 'dropped' just means that the label has decided not to trigger the next option in the contractual agreement between them and the artist, which they are legally entitled to do (even if they have triggered more than one of their previous options) because an option is not a firm commitment in the first place.

REFERENCES

ABC. (2013, February 12). *Gotye picks up three Grammys*. Retrieved February 24, 2016, from http://www.abc.net.au/news/2013-02-11/gotye-picks-up-three-grammys/4511814

Adams, C. (2014, October 20). Producer Styalz Fuego talks about the stories behind his hits with 360 and gives tips to songwriters. *News.com.au*. Retrieved February 24, 2016, from http://www.news.com.au/entertainment/music/producer-styalz-fuego-talks-about-the-stories-behind-his-hits-with-360-and-gives-tips-to-songwriters/news-story/268739fe9f1bc1663d922cf55149dd40

Alberts. (2016). *The basics*. Retrieved April 7, 2016, from http://albertmusic.com/musicians/the-basics

Ankeny, J. (2016). Gotye: Biography. *iTunes Preview*. Retrieved April 7, 2016, from https://itunes.apple.com/us/artist/gotye/id161541223

Becker, H. (1982). *Art worlds*. Berkeley, CA/Los Angeles, CA: University of California Press.

Billboard.com. (2012). *Hot 100 songs & new music: 1–10 songs | Billboard music charts*. Retrieved September 16, 2012, from http://www.Billboard.com/

Bilton, C. (2007). *Management and creativity: From creative industries to creative management*. Oxford, UK: Blackwell Publishing.

Blank, S. (2013, May). Why the lean startup changes everything. *Harvard Business Review*. Retrieved February 25, 2016, from https://hbr.org/2013/05/why-the-lean-start-up-changes-everything

Blank, S., & Dorf, B. (2012). *The startup owner's manual: A step-by-step guide for building a great company*. Pescadero, CA: K&S Ranch.

Bourdieu, P. (1986). The forms of capital. In J. Richardson (Ed.), *Handbook of theory and research for the sociology of education* (pp. 241–258). New York: Greenwood Press.

Bridgstock, R. (2012). Not a dirty word: Arts entrepreneurship and higher education. *Arts and Humanities in Higher Education, 12*(2–3), 122–137.

Burnard, P. (2012). *Musical creativities in practice*. Oxford: Oxford University Press.

CDBaby.com. (2016). *CDBaby: Sell your music*. Retrieved February 18, 2016, from http://members.cdbaby.com

Chugg, M. (2010). *Hey, you in the black T-shirt: The real story of touring the world's biggest acts*. Sydney, Australia: Pan Macmillan.

Csikszentmihalyi, M. (1996). *Creativity: Flow and the psychology of discovery and invention*. New York: Harper Perennial.

Damodaran, A. (2011). *The little book of valuation: How to value a company, pick a stock and profit*. Hoboken, NJ: Wiley.

Eisenmann, T., Ries, E., & Dillard, S. (2012). Hypothesis-driven entrepreneurship: The lean startup. *Harvard Business School Entrepreneurial Management Case No. 812–095*. Retrieved February 25, 2016, from http://ssrn.com/abstract=2037237

Goodman, F. (1997). *The mansion on the hill: Dylan, Young, Geffen, Springsteen, and the head-on collision of rock and commerce*. New York: Vintage Books/Random House.

Gotye.com. (2016). *Gotye*. Retrieved February 24, 2016, from http://www.gotye.com

Graham, P. (2012). *Startup = Growth*. Retrieved February 25, 2016, from http://paulgraham.com/growth.html

Hughes, D., Keith, S., Morrow, G., Evans, M., & Crowdy, D. (2013). What constitutes artist success in the Australian music industries? *International Journal of Music Business Research, 2*(2), 61–80.

Jolly, A. (Ed.). (2003). *The European business handbook 2003.* London, UK: Kogan Page.
Jolly, N. (2011a, July 21). Ashton Kutcher gets behind Gotye. *The Music Network.* Retrieved February 9, 2012, from http://www.themusicnetwork.com/
Jolly, N. (2011b, July 25). Lily Allen joins Gotye praise chorus. *The Music Network.* Retrieved February 9, 2012, from http://www.themusicnetwork.com/
Kilgour, M. (2006). Improving the creative process: Analysis of the effects of divergent thinking techniques and domain specific knowledge on creativity. *International Journal of Business and Society, 7*(2), 79–107.
Le, P., Masse, D., & Paris, T. (2013). Technological change at the heart of the creative process: Insights from the videogame industry. *International Journal of Arts Management, 15*(2), 45–59.
Leblanc, L. (2015). *Industry profile: Mark Meharry.* Retrieved February 20, 2016, from http://celebrityaccess.com/members/profile.html?id=693&PHPSESSID=83qno8e9fl9hmcd1t6g6t8cqd7
Lindvall, H. (2012). How music lovers lose out from fan-to-fan ticket exchanges. *The Guardian.* Retrieved February 20, 2016, from http://www.theguardian.com/media/2012/nov/28/fan-to-fan-ticket-exchanges
Madden, C., & Bloom, T. (2001). Advocating creativity. *International Journal of Cultural Policy, 7*(3), 409–436.
Madden, C., & Bloom, T. (2004). Creativity, health and arts advocacy. *International Journal of Cultural Policy, 10*(2), 133–156.
Morrow, G. (2006). *Managerial creativity: A study of artist management practices in the Australian popular music industry.* Unpublished PhD thesis, Macquarie University, Sydney, Australia.
Morrow, G. (2011). Sync agents and artist managers: A scarcity of attention and an abundance of onscreen attention. *Screen Sound, 2,* 104–117.
Mulligan, B. (2010). Brenden Mulligan: Avoid DIY sites that do too much. *Midemblog.* Retrieved February 18, 2016, from http://blog.midem.com/2010/11/brenden-mulligan-avoid-diy-sites-that-do-too-much/
Mumford, M. (2003). Where have we been, where are we going? Taking stock in creativity research. *Creativity Research Journal, 15*(2–3), 107–120.
Mumford & Sons. (2015a). To all our fans around the world: Help us to stop the ticket touts. *Mumford & Sons.* Retrieved February 20, 2016, from http://www.mumfordandsons.com/news/to-all-our-fans-around-the-world-help-us-to-stop-the-ticket-touts/
Mumford & Sons. (2015b). Mumford & Sons chat about the 2015 Stopover Festivals. *Stopover Festivals.* Retrieved February 20, 2016, from http://www.gentlemenoftheroad.com/stopovers/about/ http://www.mumfordandsons.com/news/gentlemen-of-the-road-stopovers-2015/
Mumford & Sons. (2016). *Home.* Retrieved February 20, 2016, from http://www.mumfordandsons.com/

Music Glue. (2015) *About Music Glue*. Retrieved February 20, 2016, from https://www.musicglue.com/about/
Music Glue. (2016). *Music Glue* [tweets]. Retrieved February 20, 2016, from https://twitter.com/musicglue?lang=en
Music Glue. (n.d.). *Artist features*. Retrieved February 20, 2016, from https://www.musicglue.com/services/
Negus, K. (1992). *Producing pop*. London, UK: Edward Arnold.
Negus, K., & Pickering, M. (2000). Creativity and cultural production. *International Journal of Cultural Policy, 6*(2), 259–282.
NME. (2013). Mumford & Sons call Olympic Park gig 'shitloads better than Glastonbury'. Retrieved August 2, 2016, from, http://www.nme.com/news/mumford-and-sons/71287
Ots, M., & Hartmann, B. J. (2015). Media brand cultures: Researching and theorizing how consumers engage in the social construction of media brands. In G. Siegert, K. Förster, S. Chan-Olmsted, & M. Ots (Eds.), *Handbook of media branding*. Cham, Switzerland: Springer.
Pareles, J. (2011, October 22). Gotye fans turn out to sing along. *The New York Times*. Retrieved February 9, 2012, from http://artsbeat.blogs.nytimes.com/2011/10/22/gotye-fans-turn-out-to-sing-along/?_r=0
Ries, E. (2011). *The lean startup*. New York: Crown Business.
Robinson, F. (2001). *A proven methodology to maximize return on risk*. Retrieved February 24, 2016, from http://www.syncdev.com/minimum-viable-product/
Robinson, T. (2009). Mark Meharry from Music Glue [Interview]. *BBC Introducing: Fresh On The Net*. Retrieved February 20, 2016, from http://freshonthenet.co.uk/2009/04/mark-meharry-from-music-glue/
Sisario, B. (2011, October 2). Online tools help bands do business. *The New York Times*. Retrieved February 18, 2016, from http://www.nytimes.com/2011/10/03/business/media/high-tech-tools-help-bands-market-directly-to-fans.html?pagewanted=1&_r=3&sq=topspin%20media&st=cse&scp=1
Smith, G. (2013). Seeking 'success' in popular music. *Music Education Research International, 6,* 26–37.
Thompson, K. (1998). It's the future, baby: How CD baby helps indie musicians with digital distribution. *Future of Music Coalition*. Retrieved February 18, 2016, from https://futureofmusic.org/article/its-future-baby
Thornton, S. (2006). Understanding hipness: 'Subcultural Capital' as feminist tool. In A. Bennett, B. Shank, & J. Toynbee (Eds.), *The popular music studies reader* (pp. 99–105). New York: Routledge.
Throsby, D., & Zednik, A. (2011). Multiple job-holding and artistic careers: Some empirical evidence. *Cultural Trends, 20*(1), 9–24.

Top40-Charts.com. (n.d.). *Gotye & Kimbra*. Retrieved February 20, 2016, from http://top40-charts.com/artist.php?aid=12912
Twitter.com. (2011). Twitter / MrsLRCooper : Love this video.... *Lily Allen*. Retrieved February 9, 2012, from https://twitter.com/lilyrosecooper/status/94463921272004608.
Walters, M. (2015). *How I got here*. Retrieved February 6, 2016, from http://www.parlourgigs.com/blog/2015/2/23/how-i-got-here
Watson, J. (2013). *Keynote Q & A with John Watson*. Interviewed by N. Megel on 12 September 2013, BigSound, The Judith Wright Centre, Brisbane, Australia.
Weisberg, R. (2006). *Creativity: Understanding innovation in problem solving, science, invention, and the arts*. Hoboken, NJ: Wiley.
Weisberg, R. (2010). The study of creativity: From genius to cognitive science. *International Journal of Cultural Policy, 16*(3), 235–253.
West, A. (2015). *Music Glue: Founder Mark Meharry discusses the online service that aims to shake up music industry*. Retrieved February 20, 2016, from http://www.ibtimes.co.uk/music-glue-founder-mark-meharry-discusses-online-service-that-aims-shake-music-industry-1500683
Williamson, J., & Cloonan, M. (2007). Rethinking the music industry. *Popular Music, 26*(2), 305–322.
Wiseman-Trowse, N. (2008). *Performing class in British popular music*. Basingstoke, UK: Palgrave Macmillan.
Youtube. (2013a). *Top 100 most viewed YouTube videos [Apr. 2013]*. Retrieved April 7, 2016, from https://www.youtube.com/watch?v=P_YZ_Of6xng&nohtml5=False
Youtube. (2013b). *Top 25 most liked YouTube videos (Jul. 2013)*. Retrieved April 7, 2016, from https://www.youtube.com/watch?v=txtu_1Doevk&nohtml5=False

CHAPTER 4

Creativities, Production Technologies and Song Authorship

Abstract This chapter addresses new concepts of musical creativities, collaborations and contemporary forms of musical authorship. It therefore focuses on diverse creativities and challenges the traditional notion of 'creativity'. In this context, the crafting of songs, the authorship of songs and the use of technologies that assist in the crafting process are outlined. The ways in which the democratisation of technologies (such as recording software) has resulted in a range of artistic options and practices in music production is also discussed, and new options in networked creativity, co-writing and collaborations are considered. The chapter concludes with discussion of the fusion of narratives.

Keywords Song • Songwriting • Musical authorship • Music production • Collaboration

In popular music, the creative process involving the authorship of a song is usually thought of as following one of two possible approaches: top-tier or grass-roots. In top-tier pop music, songwriting teams—consisting of lyricists, vocalists, instrumentalists, composers, producers, and so on—create rough demos of a song. A publisher then offers these demos to various artists, their labels, or their management teams, and the artists then perform and record the song themselves. A top-tier artist may also be co-opted to co-write songs by labels and/or publishers. The second approach is more commonly found in rock, singer-songwriter and acoustic genres; the

© The Editor(s) (if applicable) and The Author(s) 2016
D. Hughes et al., *The New Music Industries*,
DOI 10.1007/978-3-319-40364-9_4

artists themselves, often alongside their bandmates, will write the song and lyrics and will perform and/or record it at home, in a studio or some other location and in a variety of formats for multiple platforms.

In each of these scenarios the division of labour is fairly well understood. There are those who write music, those who play or perform it and those who record it, and the process usually happens in that order. One person may fulfil multiple roles, but these areas are typically understood to be distinct from each other. These various functions are reflected in music industries' and copyright terminology; songwriter, lyricist, arranger, performer and studio producer, each with its own (partial) claim to authorship of a song. These roles, however, were developed not because they accurately define the process of artistic creativity, but because they assist in determining intellectual ownership of the song and in dispensing songwriting royalties. The actual artistic creativities are more complex, and involve many factors external to the studio. For example, authors themselves draw influence (consciously or subconsciously) from a wide variety of sources, particularly via the Internet, and might draw on others' creativity by creating works that are covers of existing works or by incorporating audio samples of existing works.

Other areas are also vague, such as the distinction between performers and authors. Performer rights are separate from author rights; in Australia, authors retain copyright over the song itself, while performers retain rights over specific recordings (Australian Copyright Council, 2014). A person in the role of performer may, however, contribute significantly to the song itself by way of unplanned extemporisations, or by working alongside the songwriter and producer during recording, which may not be recognised in the writing credits. Moreover, the studio producer, and even the mixing or mastering engineer, occupies a broad role and may or may not be actively involved in songwriting; simultaneously, songwriters themselves are increasingly using production technology during the writing process. Remixes, covers, versions and sampling, enabled and legitimised through web technologies and social media, further challenge 'traditional' notions of authorship and artistic creativity. These scenarios show the limitations of considering artistic creativity, including musical authorship, as a clinical practice where neat boundaries can be drawn around its constituent parts.

This chapter addresses contemporary forms of authorship and creativities in popular music, with attention to some of the changes to the music industries and music production in recent years. It focuses on the careers of contemporary musical artists, and will draw on interviews with several artists and those in related sectors of the industries (management, copyright collection, publishing, and so on) to relate artistic creativity to current practices. In particular, it outlines some of the complexities of creative practice for musicians in the Internet era.

The Crafting of Songs

Popular music and creativity in general have historically been understood in the Western world as an undertaking that involves the creator artistically expressing a unique persona or perspective through song or other creative media. In popular culture, this results in a tendency to position creative figures as individual artists, who produce their works following some kind of 'mystical' inspiration, as Sternberg terms it (1999, p. 5). This is despite the concept that many popular singers are the public face of top-tier songwriting processes.

The prevailing individualistic view of creativity has been criticised, most notably by Csikzentmihalyi (2014). Reminiscent of elements of Bourdieu's cultural theory (Bourdieu, 1993), in a collection of his works Csikzentmihalyi (2014) proposes that creativity arises from the interaction of three forces (*domain, field* and the *individual*), an interaction that recognises that multiple factors are needed in order for creativity to take place (p. 47). The *domain* consists of skills or knowledge relevant to an area (Csikzenmihalyi, 2014, p. 47); for popular music songwriting, this may include instrumental ability, musical theory, awareness of genre and style, and various technical skills. *Field* describes the actors that consume and assess creative works, including other artists, audiences, and institutional figures (Csikzenmihalyi, 2014, p. 47). The *individual* negotiates and responds to the field and domain in order to produce creative works (Csikzenmihalyi, 2014, p. 47). Similarly, Hennessey and Amabile (2010) noted that creativity is defined on a variety of levels, from the microscopic neurological level, to the individual level, to the holistic systems level proposed by Csikzentmihalyi (2014). However, this more nuanced depiction of creativity does not negate the existence of musical creativity as process and songwriting as a typically highly personal pursuit. The following quote by Jenny Biddle (singer-songwriter) highlights the interpersonal and audience-focused elements of performance and artistic creative practice:

> I don't want to write a song for the sake of a hit song; I want to feel and connect with people, I want to entertain. I really love those gigs where there

might be 60 people in a room and you can look at each and every one of them and pull faces and they laugh, and they cry, and they tell stories. I love those gigs.

The individual-focused definition of the 'liberal artist' (Wiseman-Trowse, 2008, p. 42) endures, particularly in discussions of authenticity. 'Authentic' songwriters are driven by self-expression and by the pursuit of music itself as an artform, rather than approaching songwriting as a mechanical process that takes into account the demands or desires of the field, or commercial concerns. As discussed previously, this notion is fundamentally undermined when the artist is income driven or an artist-entrepreneur, and yet this viewpoint is often expressed by musicians themselves, as shown in Jenny Biddle's words above. The idea of not 'writing a song for the sake of a hit song' points to anxieties around the relationship between individual creativity and the domain/field, particularly that between music and commerce, as explored by Negus (1999).

As early as the mid twentieth century, Adorno's (1941) zealous criticism of popular music focused on the detrimental 'standardisation' of music wrought by the industrial nature of pop music production. Yet, as McIntyre (2012, p. 168) pointed out, the valorisation of the individual songwriter-performer is a comparatively recent phenomenon, arising in the 1950s. It occurred largely in response to the growing phenomenon of teen and youth culture, as teenagers were more likely to accept performers who they perceived as being like themselves (McIntyre, 2012, p. 168). Artists and songwriters, whether consciously or subconsciously, began to embody the required authenticity in their creative work; this occurs to a lesser extent in some pop music, but is a cornerstone of many genres including singer-songwriter, rock, and indie.

Authorship

The concept of authorship is tied to both creativity and authenticity. It defines a creator's ownership of an artefact, and describes the creative process with regard to larger social systems. Burnard (2012), drawing on the work of Csikzentmihalyi (1999) and Bourdieu (1993), situates authorship as a social process which articulates the creator's position socially, stating that composers 'can only exist or be known as such through the social discourses and practices in which they are constituted,' (Burnard, 2012, p. 226). She goes on to discern 'self-social' and 'sociocultural' forms of authorship; the first describes creativity as a personal or interpersonal undertaking, and the second describes creativity in relation to established scenes or traditions (2012, p. 226).

As discussed in the previous chapter, 'branding' a band or an artist is an idea that has become more prominent in recent years as artists are increasingly able (or obliged) to manage their own marketing and promotions through social media. As one digital music specialist (name withheld) explained, 'From day one, bands are creating their brand without realising it. Their image creates their brand, their music creates their brand, their logo creates their brand.' Likewise, Joel Connolly (artist manager) stated: 'As soon as you decide to try and make a living off your music or take it outside of your bedroom and share it with an audience then it becomes a product and a product is a brand.'

By creating a distinct brand, artists clarify their authorship, situating themselves in relation to a particular genre and practice (self-social authorship), while declaring their position with respect to existing institutions and broader social influences such as fans, labels, and promoters (socio-cultural authorship). While many other forms of authorship (see Burnard, 2012) exist, branding provides a useful lens to explore artists' authorial process. Additionally, the currency of social media as a unified platform for promoting, marketing, disseminating and selling music, video and images, reinforces the link between music and product, connecting artistic and commercial aspects of creativity.

These brief and broad discussions show the complex creativities that need to be negotiated by current musical artists. Leaving aside the creative process underpinning the actual musical work, artists need to balance broader cultural expectations with commercial concerns, and need to define their identities in order to reach a global and fragmented consumer base.

Technologies that have Changed Creativity/ Authorship

Contemporary music artists negotiate a complex landscape of commercial and cultural concerns in their creative practice. Aside from the long-standing tensions surrounding authenticity (see Barker & Taylor, 2007; Weisethaunet & Lindberg, 2010; McIntyre, 2012), technological changes have also significantly changed the field and domain of creativity. Expanding on Burnard's (2012) exploration of musical creativities' technological mediations, a host of technologies for recording, producing, communicating, performing, collaborating and selling music have reshaped contemporary musicians' practices.

The fracturing of the music industries and development of web technologies that foster DIY musicians has meant that, alongside musical skills, artists are increasingly required to be proficient in (or, at least, aware of) a range of other areas. One such area is music production technology; digital audio workstations, audio recording, MIDI sequencing, synthesisers, and sampling are often used in songwriting, and are becoming more and more accessible and affordable. These are not simply tools required for recording; they can also alter the creative process itself, leading to new workflows and creative results.

Non-musical technical skills are also important, including use of social media and broader computer skills. A general awareness of trends, the field of popular music and management skills are also necessary, as these allow the musician to effectively interact with an audience. Communicating with the field (after Csikzentmihalyi, 2014) has likewise been affected by technology. Musicians are more connected globally, rather than locally, and are (in principle) able to reach significant international audiences with minimal outlay. Similarly, musicians are able to draw influence from, and connect with, a wider variety of other artists. This fundamental shift to online is addressed by Liz Tripodi (vocal teacher, entrepreneur, and performer) who stated: 'There was no social media 20 years ago. These days if you're not trying to put your hands in as many different pies as possible, you have no chance of making any sort of career in the industry'.

The online space has also radically reconfigured the music industries; instead of record labels, services such as YouTube, Facebook and Spotify are key curators of content. Moreover, fans and audiences now have control over artists' online presences. Whereas in the pre-Internet era record labels were held responsible for breaching artists' moral rights by intervening in the work's integrity, fans today may breach the artist's moral rights or affect their online presence by uploading videos to sites such as YouTube.

As sales revenues from recordings continue to diminish (IFPI, 2015, p. 7), other revenue streams have become more important, such as those relating to synchronisation, live performance, sponsorship, crowdsourcing and merchandising. Technology has also changed the way music is listened to, with album sales declining in favour of individual songs and user-compiled playlists (Paxson, 2010, p. 84). Artist marketing strategies have also shifted towards social media and other means; in addition to maintaining a constant online presence, artists pursue collaborations (often internationally) and synchronisations in order to sustain their careers. These changes have impacted artists at all levels, from the beginning independent musician to well-established, top-level artists such as Ed Sheeran. For instance, Sheeran is ambivalent about the financial reward of recorded music and streaming services such as Spotify, stating, 'I'm in the music industry to play live... This album [x] (Asylum/Atlantic, 2014) was streamed 26 million times in the first week on Spotify... That means a tenth of them might consider buying a ticket or going to a festival, and that's enough for me to tour very comfortably' (cited in Dredge, 2014); he also distributes a free EP to fans via his website in exchange for their email address (Asylum Records, 2014). Sheeran has also partnered with Pepsi and Clear Channel (Hampp, 2014) to promote his album x, and Nokia (Hampp, 2013) to film a music video using the Nokia Lumia 928 mobile phone. The 2012 video for 'Give Me Love' (written by Sheeran, Gosling, and Leonard, 2012) partnered with the social video app Vyclone, combining fans' video footage of Sheeran in concert into a single official video using hundreds of fans' perspectives (Asylum Records, 2014). Collaboration and synchronisation has also been important throughout Sheeran's career, including co-writes for UK-based pop group One Direction and solo artist Olly Murs (Lindner, 2015), collaboration with other artists including Taylor Swift, Rudimental and The Weeknd (as well as a 2011 EP titled 'No. 5 Collaborations' featuring collaborations with a number of UK-based grime artists), and synchronization on television shows including *The Vampire Diaries* and *Grey's Anatomy* (IMDB.com, 2016). Artists like Sheeran are less likely to be personally involved in activities such as day-to-day management of social media (in fact, Sheeran is taking a year-long personal hiatus from social media in 2016 (Instagram, 2015)) and to a large extent still rely on the album-tour cycle. However, artists or their management participate in continual engagement with audiences (via traditional or online media); for example, Taylor Swift's former manager Rick Barker suggested that artists should post on Twitter between five to ten times per day and YouTube once a week (Social Media for Music, 2015).

The effect of these developments on artists' creativity is far-reaching. More than ever before, musicians are able to connect with distant audiences and peers, listen to a wide variety of music and produce high-quality musical works without needing to first secure substantial funding to hire a studio or additional personnel. Using social media, artists can also be actively involved in their own marketing, management and development. At the same time, these musicians must maintain, or portray, their own authenticity in line with the expectations of genre and audience.

Musical creativities (songwriting, producing and recording) and non-musical creativities (branding, audience engagement and image-making) are increasingly overlapping areas.

Such a coming together of artistic creativities and managerial or economic concerns resonates with McGuigan's (2009) notion of 'cool capitalism' and the way in which individualist bourgeois values are reinforced by capitalist cultural aspects. The perception that record labels and 'the industry' restrict the artist's 'true self' through market fundamentalism is challenged by contemporary DIY artists, who are now directly concerned about the market themselves. This has changed the way in which artists construct their authenticity in relation to, and against, the market. The following section explores three areas of note in considering changing musical creativities; production technology, networked creativity and covers.

Production Technologies and Creativities

The availability of consumer-oriented music production equipment and computer applications has patently made music more affordable to record and produce. The growth of 'prosumer' (Toffler 1984) music producers has been acknowledged for many years, and now is well embedded in everyday practice, with prominent 'bedroom producers' such as Flume[1] receiving widespread critical acclaim. As one digital music strategist (name withheld) put it, 'Anyone with a laptop and the right software can feasibly create their own music, and quality music, if they know what they're doing and they know how to use the software.' The pre-digital career progression of a band recording a rough demo, approaching a label, recording an album, and debuting to a wider audience has to an extent been reversed; today, artists need to distribute and/or perform high-quality music to reach a following, then demonstrate this following (via numerous Facebook 'likes', for example) in order to approach a label. This circular model has had several effects on artists' creative practices.

One of these effects is the changing role of the song. As artists are increasingly able to self-produce both audio and video material, and audiences' consumption habits are becoming more oriented towards individual songs rather than albums, there is a tendency toward a continuous release of material in order to engage with audiences. Moreover, the song, as a standalone audio recording, is no longer sufficient, as Matt Amery (artist) noted: 'If we wanted to get played on [national radio station] triple j now, what we'd need to do is make sure you're on blogs and on tastemaker sites and to do that you need to have a video clip to show who you are and what you're all about. Rather than just a song it needs to be a whole package.' This strategy involves significant financial outlay by the artist as well as commitment to a brand, meaning visual aspects and overall creative direction. Dean Ormston (Head of Member Services Group for collecting society APRA AMCOS) likewise underlines the need for artists to have a high degree of self-awareness early on in their careers, and to consider their overall creative position and career trajectory when songwriting.

Production practices have also changed owing to the revenue streams available to artists today. Whereas (physical) album sales were once a significant source of revenue for artists, the digital model of continual engagement favours singles. The single-based digital economy, furthermore, uses music as a free tool for engagement and data collection rather than a source of revenue, and this operating model enables fans to stream music in exchange for personal information such as their email address. Likewise, the shift towards video rather than audio-only releases reflects platforms such as YouTube as potential revenue sources.

Another revenue stream from recorded media is commercial music streaming where revenue returns to artists can be viewed as being 'ridiculously low', as one interviewee described it. Synchronisation, particularly in advertising, is a growing revenue stream and, to an extent, is replacing the role of recorded music; as Matt Amery noted, syncs for his music have 'outweighed anything that we have sold'. This has led to the writing of songs particularly for synchronisation, a practice that is sometimes criticised when alluding to the conflict between authenticity and potential profit-seeking in songwriting.

The examples above show the far-reaching effects of technology on musical creativity. Aside from more noticeable technological mediations such as recording music on mobile phones, swapping samples online or using portable mp3 players, as discussed by Burnard (2012), technological changes affecting the music industries also have a profound impact on the creative practices of artists. This can be seen in the shift towards video as an important creative output, the need to claim authorship by actively branding early in one's career, and orientation towards more diverse revenue streams.

Networked Creativity: Co-writing and Collaboration

Technology has also affected creative practices related to songwriting. Artists themselves can discover new music (and be discovered themselves) through websites and streaming services such as iTunes and Apple Music,

Spotify, Facebook, YouTube and so on. This facility, as well as the ability to easily and quickly communicate online, has led to new possibilities for collaboration between artists; as Dean Ormston noted: 'There isn't any sense at all of just thinking about making something just here in Australia—it's teaming up with the best in the world to do whatever it is that you are doing today.' This was echoed by statements noting the relevance of international audiences in building sustainable careers. Another way that artists can actively target international audiences is through co-writing songs, as raised by Dean Ormston, who stated: 'The way to break into a new market might be to collaborate with a local artist, because you're already in a certain part of Asia or wherever, rather than relying solely on the traditional model of trying to 'break' the band.'

The practice of co-writing and collaboration is particularly pronounced in electronic music and DJ releases, where producers will typically formulate the underlying beat and arrangement, then pass it on to a top line writer who devises the main melody, vocal line, and lyrics. As Martin Novosel (label manager) explains, 'Most of the time with publishing, it is shared with co-writers, because in my experience DJ producers rarely write top lines.' Collaborations are increasingly popular and this approach is particularly important for songwriters and music publishing. Robert Scott (Founder of Source Music Publishing and Licensing and Creative Manager, Embassy Music Publishing Music Sales) used the number of Swedish songwriters in the US music market to illustrate the growing internationalisation of songwriting. He further stated, 'I have tried to talk to my songwriters and get them to reach out and talk to other songwriters in other territories, because it is all about opening up all the possibilities.'

The Internet has contributed to artists' practices in several ways, as noted by Burnard (2012, p. 226), including sample-swapping and crowdsourced projects. The sharing and liking economy of social media sites is another Internet-based technological change affecting songwriting and collaboration. Social media is most commonly used by artists as a means for communicating with their fans, but also allows artists to find and work with others. Penny Pettigrew (artist) noted the potential of social media for fostering collaboration and has had other musicians encourage collaborations between herself and other artists, recounting, 'I have had amazing musicians share my Facebook page… [saying] please, if you need a singer, go to her.'

The above scenarios show how the Internet has changed not only music distribution and consumption practices, but even songwriting itself. As artists increasingly compete in a global marketplace, regularly produce and distribute music online, and have access to other artists via social media, co-writing and collaborating are becoming valuable tools for reaching new audiences and building a sustainable career.

MEMETIC CREATIVITY: THE NEW COVERS

A further effect of Internet technology on musical creativity is the growing practice of musical cover videos. Like co-writing and collaboration, covering others' musical works is a way to expand an audience and to participate in current trends and memes. Musical covers, cover bands and tribute artists (who endeavour to exactly replicate other artists' appearance and mannerisms) are well established in popular music (see Homan, 2006; Cusic, 2005; Beebe, Fulbrook & Saunders, 2002). Homan (2006) discussed the phenomenon of the cover musician as 'a single musician, or group of musicians, that perform a range of others' material, in many instances singling out a particular era or genre for display' (p. 4), but online and social media have added further dimensions to the practice of covering. In recent years, the phenomenon of YouTube cover videos has been widely acknowledged (Burgess, 2008; Vernallis, 2013, p. 190), and many online music videos have experienced an additional wave of popularity through user-created covers. Gotye's 'Somebody That I Used To Know' (written by De Backer, 2011) and Beyonce's 'Single Ladies' (written by Stewart, Nash, Harrell, and Knowles, 2008) are two prime cases; the 2013 *Harlem Shake* meme offers a different example, being a user-generated comedy video rather than an original music video for the song 'Harlem Shake' (written by Baauer, 2012). The potential of music videos to 'snowball' into viral phenomena was remarked on by Robert Scott:

> 'The best thing to do is launch something that is so visually striking and so aurally strong that then other people want to cover it. Then it just feeds on itself and goes ballistic.' In this environment, covering an existing work is no longer solely an artist practice; it is a creative practice that can be participated in by fans, which has the effect of contributing further to the artist's currency online in terms of views, clicks, or likes. Covers, as a form of creative production, are placed towards the 'soft' side of the creativity continuum (see Chapter 1), as artists are building on and replicating established successes by other artists. Nonetheless they are a valid creative and business tool that many artists use in various contexts, as discussed below.

Online, artists can use covers strategically to attract new audiences. As Cusic (2005, p. 174) writes, 'from an artist's perspective, covers are important because they (1) provide a song proven to be a hit to the repertoire, (2) show an important influence on the artist, and (3) give the audience something familiar when introducing a new act'. An element of novelty is also required to attract viewers; where novelty is substantial or engaging, the act of covering moves further towards the 'hard' side of the creativity continuum. The covers of musical works online that draw the most views are thus often those which resituate the original work in a different genre. One example of a viral cover crossover is singer-songwriter and electronica artist Chet Faker's cover of 'No Diggity', originally by R'n'B group Blackstreet (written by Hannibal, Riley, Stewart, Walters, Young, Vick, and Withers, 1996). The track was later used in a 2013 Superbowl commercial in the USA in a lucrative synchronisation deal (AAP, 2013). Similarly, electronica producer Flume's reversioning of Yolanda Be Cool's 'A Baru In New York' (written by Handley, Stanley, and Yunupingu, 2013), featuring indigenous singer-songwriter Gurrumul, was significantly more popular than the original. Several artists have risen to prominence through the medium of YouTube covers, such as US-based group Boyce Avenue, who specialise in acoustic covers of popular songs, and UK-based singer Birdy, whose cover of Bon Iver's 'Skinny Love' (written by Vernon, 2008) has so far received close to 100 million views on YouTube. Both Boyce Avenue and Birdy now produce original material, but maintain releases of covers on YouTube.

By releasing cover versions of existing tracks, artists can ensure a flow of listeners who are already familiar with the original track; once a consistent listenership is established, the artist can then release their own original work. This lessens the distinction between original musicians and cover musicians, as outlined by Homan (2006, p. 4), and situates covering as a practice which can be engaged in strategically and sporadically, rather than as a distinct genre in and of itself. YouTube's revenue model is also worth considering; since content uploaders are paid per view, capitalising on the success of an existing song is a useful way to ensure some views, and therefore income. Additionally, YouTube's Content ID recognition system identifies when a song is used in a video, providing artists with performance royalties (provided they are registered with a collection agency) and mechanical royalties each time a song is used. This provides another means for generating income for artists whose recordings or songs are used in others' videos.

It is worth noting that offline the role of covers is markedly different. Dr Daniel Robinson (artist and educator) has expressed concern about the proliferation of covers on YouTube, where 'you stand in front of the microphone with headphones on and you sing a pop cover', noting that this does not necessarily equate to live performance ability or a sustainable music career. Performing covers live is done for reasons markedly different from those for videorecording covers to distribute cover performances online (see Homan, 2006; Morrow, 2006). In the research interviews conducted by the authors, the difficulty of performing original material live was often noted, and artists reported often performing covers to satisfy risk-averse venues. It was also identified that live performance opportunities have diminished in recent years, particularly for original bands. There appear to be several causes for this, including legislative changes, alternate revenue models (such as poker machines), and changes in leisure culture (Johnson & Homan, 2002, p. 1). Jenny Biddle (singer-songwriter) explained that covers form a cornerstone of her live performance: 'I do a lot of cover gigs to pay the bread and butter, but there are original pieces in there as well.'

In regional areas particularly, Leanne de Souza (artist manager) noted, 'it's basically covers bands or nothing. [We're having difficulty] finding a place that will put on an original band and an original emerging band.' Still, Jenny Biddle noted that she uses cover shows 'to get my chops up in terms of musicianship and performing skills and interacting with audiences', and also that she intersperses covers with her own original music.

Online, covers provide a means for artists to connect with new audiences and with other artists. In particular, well-considered cross-genre collaborations can result in innovative musical works that appeal to a wide listener base. Meanwhile, covers in live performance are often played out of necessity owing to the growing preference for covers by venues that was identified by Leanne de Souza above, yet still offer musicians an opportunity to practice their skills in front of a live audience. Both of these circumstances show how musical creativity is a networked process, as artists need awareness of the current musical landscape in order to successfully produce work that resonates with audiences.

A Fusion of Narratives

Singer-songwriters typically relate personal narrative (self-social) or they craft a song around the narrative of others (sociocultural). The creative practice of singer-songwriter Passenger[2] (Mike Rosenberg) does both. Passenger traverses continents, incorporates street-to-stage performances and highlights a grass-roots approach to crafting and sharing his songs.

His creative practice, banter and audience engagement are grounded in busking traditions. An analysis of Passenger's body of work including large[3] and small[4] venue performances, interviews and recordings, identifies that was *in* and *through* busking locations and encounters with audiences that Passenger, the artist, emerged along with many of his songs.

Within the tradition afforded by socio-spatial interconnectivity, busking provided Passenger with the place in which to develop and perform his music. As a result, he often conveys site-specific narratives (for example, 'All the Little Lights', written by Rosenberg, 2012), sociocultural experiences (for example, 'I Hate', written by Rosenberg, 2012) and audience interactions (for example, 'Holes', written by Rosenberg, 2012). He also retells the stories of other people whom he met through chance encounters (for example, 'Riding to New York', written by Rosenberg, 2014). Passenger creates networks across communities through an integrative narrative that includes online platforms, social media and fundraising efforts that highlight the plight of some communities. In relation to the sale of *Whispers Two* (Nettwerk/Black Crow, 2015), for example, Passenger noted on the accompanying booklet/sleeve (the following excerpt is as written):

> so i have decided to give all profits from every sale of 'whispers two' to unicef – more specifically their campaign to help and eventually prevent children suffering from chronic malnutrition in liberia. one of the poorest countries on the planet… money raised from these sales will go directly towards food and supplements to help bring severely malnourished kids back to health, facility upgrades and maintenance, education and training for health workers in the region. (Rosenberg, 2015)

While sociocultural authorship fuses narratives in song, so do fundraising efforts related to a particular song, as the example above highlights. Another recent example is Tim Minchin's song 'Come Home (Cardinal Pell)' (Minchin, 2016a), which is a satirical response to Cardinal Pell's inability to return to Australia to give evidence at the Australian Royal Commission on Child Abuse (Minchin, 2016b). Proceeds from the sale of the single assist victims to fly to Rome and attend Pell's otherwise relayed evidence statement:

> Proceeds from its sale will go into this fund: GoFundMe—Send Ballarat Survivors to Rome. You can buy it worldwide now from iTunes or Google Play and you can stream it on Apple Music or Spotify. GoFundMe—Send Ballarat Survivors To Rome. (Minchin, 2016b)

Conclusion

The above explorations question the entrenched divide between musical creativity (namely songwriting, including instrumental proficiency, musicianship, lyrical expertise and so on) and what might be termed *paramusical* creativity (after Tagg, 1986). Paramusical creativity involves the musical artist responding to his or her wider circumstances, and is affected by technological developments, economic factors, and broader cultural trends. For example, the development of consumer-level production technology has made it easier for artists to self-produce music, as both audio and music video. But the deeper effect of this development is that artists now release music more frequently, accompanied by video, in order to continuously engage with their audience. The type of music being released to audiences has also changed; instead of a professionally produced album, artists now focus at the song-level and below; they may release impromptu acoustic recordings, covers of other artists' songs, videos of live performances or demo versions of songs. Similarly, the economic changes to the music industries (namely, the decline in revenues from recorded work) have compelled artists to focus more on the other income streams that were outlined in Chapter 2, and to adjust their creative practices accordingly, through actively seeking collaboration with other artists, or by pursuing synchronisation as a revenue stream. Among these wider forces, artists need to actively differentiate themselves and assert their authorship, self-brand, and engage across multiple media types and platforms, producing videos, images and audio to maintain a constant level of communication with their audience.

Notes

1. Flume (Harley Streten) is an Australian producer who in 2013 was nominated for a record eight ARIAs (Australian Recording Industry Awards) for his debut album *Flume*, which reached #1 on Apple's iTunes charts. He began producing using free software (FL Studio) and produces in a laptop-based studio (Future Music, 2014).
2. See http://passengermusic.com.
3. An example is Passenger's performance on 23 January 2015, at the Qantas Credit Union Arena, Sydney, Australia. The Qantas Credit Union Arena closed in December 2015, but was capable of accommodating 12,000 people. See http://www.austadiums.com/stadiums/stadiums.php?id=114.

4. An example is Passenger's performance on 24 February 2015, at the Enmore Theatre, Sydney, Australia. The theatre is art deco in construction. See http://www.enmoretheatre.com.au.

REFERENCES

AAP. (2013, February 1). Hot Diggity! Melbourne musician gets $4m Super Bowl slot. *Sydney Morning Herald*. Retrieved February 18, 2016, from http://www.smh.com.au/entertainment/music/hot-diggity-melbourne-musician-gets-4m-super-bowl-slot-20130201-2dpeo.html

Adorno, T. W. (1941). On popular music. *Studies in Philosophy and Social Science, IX*, 17–48.

Asylum Records. (2014). Ed needs you! Be part of the film crew. *EdSheeran.com*. Retrieved February 19, 2016, from http://www.edsheeran.com/vyclone

Australian Copyright Council. (2014). *Music & Copyright*. Retrieved January 27, 2016, from http://www.copyright.org.au/acc_prod/ACC/Information_Sheets/Music___Copyright.aspx

Barker, H., & Taylor, Y. (2007). *Faking it: The quest for authenticity in popular music*. New York: W. W. Norton & Company.

Beebe, R., Fulbrook, D., & Saunders, B. (Eds.). (2002). *Rock over the edge: Transformations in popular music culture*. Durham, NC: Duke University Press.

Bourdieu, P. (1993). *The field of cultural production: Essays on art and literature*, R. Johnson (Ed). Cambridge, UK: Polity Press.

Burgess, J. (2008). All your chocolate rain are belong to us? Viral video, YouTube and the dynamics of participatory culture. In G. Lovink (Ed.), *Video Vortex reader: Responses to YouTube* (pp. 101–109). Amsterdam, The Netherlands: Institute of Network Cultures.

Burnard, P. (2012). *Musical creativities in practice*. Oxford, UK: Oxford University Press.

Csikzentmihalyi, M. (1999). Implications of a systems perspective for the study of creativity. In R. Sternberg (Ed.), *Handbook of creativity* (pp. 313–335). New York: Cambridge University Press.

Csikzentmihalyi, M. (2014). *The systems model of creativity: The collected works of Mihaly Csikszentmihalyi*. Dordrecht, The Netherlands: Springer.

Cusic, D. (2005). In defense of cover songs. *Popular Music and Society, 28*(2), 171–177.

Dredge, S. (2014), Ed Sheeran talks Spotify royalties: 'I'm in the music industry to play live…'. *Guardian News and Media*. Retrieved February 19, 2016, from http://www.theguardian.com/technology/2014/sep/30/ed-sheeran-spotify-streaming

Future Music. (2014). Flume with a view. *MusicRadar.com*. Retrieved February 18, 2016, from http://www.musicradar.com/news/tech/in-pictures-flumes-sydney-studio-597256

Hampp, A. (2013). Nokia music expands artist partnerships with Cher Lloyd, Ed Sheeran promotions. *Billboard.com*. Retrieved February 19, 2016, from http://www.billboard.com/biz/articles/news/branding/1564979/nokia-music-expands-artist-partnerships-with-cher-lloyd-ed

Hampp, A. (2014). Ed Sheeran teams with Clear Channel, Pepsi for "x" album release party, set to play IHeartRadio Fest (Exclusive). *Billboard.com*. Retrieved February 19, 2016, from http://www.billboard.com/biz/articles/news/legal-and-management/6099328/ed-sheeran-teams-with-clear-channel-pepsi-for-x-album

Hennessey, B. A., & Amabile, T. M. (2010). Creativity. *Annual Review of Psychology, 61*, 569–598.

Homan, S. (Ed.). (2006). *Access all eras: Tribute bands and global pop culture*. Maidenhead, UK: Open University Press.

IFPI (International Federation of the Phonographic Industry). (2015). *IFPI digital music report 2015*. Retrieved December 4, 2015, http://www.ifpi.org/downloads/Digital-Music-Report-2015.pdf

IMDB.com. (2016). *Ed Sheeran*. Retrieved February 19, 2016, from http://www.imdb.com/name/nm3247828/

Instagram.com. (2015). *Teddysphotos*. Retrieved February 19, 2016, from https://www.instagram.com/p/_ONOpUkpDz/

Johnson, B., & Homan, S. (2002). *Vanishing acts: An inquiry into the state of live popular music opportunities in New South Wales*. Sydney, Australia: Australia Council for the Arts.

Lindner, E. (2015). 19 songs you didn't know Ed Sheeran wrote. *MTV.com*. Retrieved February 19, 2016, from http://www.mtv.com/news/2084071/ed-sheeran-songs/

McGuigan, J. (2009). *Cool capitalism*. London, UK: Pluto.

McIntyre, P. (2012). *Creativity and cultural production: Issues for media practice*. London, UK: Palgrave Macmillan.

Minchin, T. (2016a). *Come Home (Cardinal Pell) – Tim Minchin* [Video]. Retrieved February 20, 2016, from https://www.youtube.com/watch?v=EtHOmforqxk

Minchin, T. (2016b). Come Home – A charity single. *Tim Minchin.com*. Retrieved February 20, 2016, from http://www.timminchin.com/2016/02/16/come-home-a-charity-single-2/#more-17691

Morrow, G. (2006). Selling out or buying in? In S. Homan (Ed.), *Access all eras: Tribute bands and global pop culture* (pp. 182–197). Maidenhead, UK: Open University Press.

Negus, K. (1999). *Music genres and corporate cultures*. New York: Routledge.

Paxson, P. (2010). *Mass communications and media studies: An introduction*. New York: Continuum.

Rosenberg, M. (2015). *Whispers II* [Book accompanying CD]. Black Crow Records.

Social Media for Music. (2015). *Social Media for Music*. Retrieved February 19, 2016, from http://socialmediaformusic.com/video/

Sternberg, R. (1999). *Handbook of creativity*. Cambridge: Cambridge University Press.

Tagg, P. (1986). Musicology and the semiotics of popular music. *Semiotica*, *66*(1–3), 279–298.

Toffler, A. (1984). *The third wave*. New York: Bantam.

Vernallis, C. (2013). *Unruly media: YouTube, music video, and the new digital cinema*. New York: Oxford University Press.

Weisethaunet, H., & Lindberg, U. (2010). Authenticity revisited: The Rock Critic and the Changing Real. *Popular Music and Society*, *22*(4), 465–485.

Wiseman-Trowse, N. (2008). *Performing class in British popular music*. Basingstoke, UK: Palgrave Macmillan.

CHAPTER 5

The Realities of Practice

Abstract The realities of practice can prove extremely challenging for some artists and can lead to issues of health, safety and wellbeing. The realities discussed in this chapter include the relevance of image and branding, the significance of a support network, contractual obligations and fiduciary aspects of associated individuals or organisations. It is essential to identify and discuss the realities of practice so that consideration may be given as to how these issues might be addressed in both practice and in education. The chapter concludes with considerations for career sustainability.

Keywords Image • Time poor • Wellbeing • Networking • Career sustainability

This chapter details the realities of practice identified in our research, specifically in relation to their impact on career trajectories, expectations (artist and industries), professional practice and lived experiences. As such, this chapter explores the day-to-day practices and concerns of participants (the realities) actively engaged within the industries. While many extant discussions of the music industries focus on issues such as legal aspects and copyright, management and policy (for example, Cloonan, 2011; Simpson & Munro, 2012; Homan, Cloonan, & Cattermole, 2015, 2016), there is a growing body of literature concerning the realities of practice for creative labourers to which this chapter contributes (for example, McGuigan,

2010; Hesmondhalgh & Baker, 2011; Stahl, 2013; Cloonan, 2014). In addition to this body of literature, there are organisations such as Support Act[1] in Australia that was 'established by the music industry to provide a safety net for music professionals facing hardship' (Support Act, 2016). This chapter builds on, and seeks to contribute to, such initiatives.

Through the range of industry roles encompassed in our research, we were able to detail a variety of experiences and highlight a number of industry factors for consideration. While there is much to celebrate in the new industries, some of the practices our participants outlined are concerning. For younger artists/musicians, the realities of (often DIY) practices can be challenging; for those more established, such realities may have been negotiated through a series of compromises and/or accepted as being standard practices. These realities include career sustainability, the significance of networking, live performance challenges, recordings, image and branding, managing expectations, and workplace health and safety issues. Some issues and concerns have fiduciary implications for associated individuals or organisations, and can prove extremely challenging for some music sector workers leading to issues of health, safety and wellbeing (Hughes, Evans, Keith, & Morrow, 2014).

While there are most certainly positive elements of working in the music industries, such as the enjoyable psychological state of (creative) flow (Csikszentmihalyi, 1996), the question of 'positive emotion' (for example, Seligman, 2011) for the creative artist is an interesting one in considering its flipside (see Drus, Kozbelt, & Hughes, 2014). There is an undeniably powerful relationship between artistic creativity and emotion or 'affect' (see Madden & Bloom, 2004, p. 135). Therefore, our discussion of participants' affective experiences sits alongside our discussion of the pragmatic realities identified by our participants.

CONTEXT

The contemporary music industries are constantly evolving, and the high rate of digital disruption (creating possible situations of financial vulnerability, exploitation and risk) means that wellness considerations for music industries practitioners have immediate relevance. Until recently, much of the research into sector wellbeing has tended to focus on financial or business matters rather than on the physical or mental wellbeing of sector workers. Recent research findings (for example Hughes et al., 2014; van den Eynde, Fisher, & Sonn, 2015), however, highlight the significance of wellness issues and health concerns in the sector. Hughes et al. (2014) identified the urgent realities of contemporary music practices, which are compounded by two significant factors. The first is the compensatory measures instigated by sector workers, which may be self-administered and/or informally modelled (such as alcohol and/or drug related use/ abuse). The second is the striking absence of wellbeing and related policies in the new music industries. The latter is significant and does not appear to be limited to an Australian context. In a comparative analysis of health and safety regulations at live music events in Finland and the UK, for example, Grönberg (2010) noted a general absence of related health and safety legislation in the European Union for 'public events' (p. 33).

Despite the fact that media reports often focus on musicians' compromised health and wellbeing issues, particularly in relation to substance abuse (for example, Bobby Brown cited by Oh, 2002), addiction (for example, Amy Winehouse cited by Dunn, 2015), and exploitation and financial hardship (for example, the impact of streaming services cited by Resnikoff, 2013), the health and wellbeing of sector workers appears to be afforded little emphasis in the reality of the workplace. Hence, there is the growing body of literature concerning creative labour referenced above. In literature specifically related to the music industries, Kenny (2014a, 2014b, 2015) explores health and wellbeing issues in the music industries. Describing the rock scene as 'a volatile mix of glamour, instant wealth, risk-taking, rebellion and psychological distress' (Kenny, 2014a), Kenny identified that over six decades (1950–2010) the lifespan of a popular musician was up to 25 years shorter when compared to the general populace (2014a). She attributes this alarming sector statistic and others, including a two to seven times greater suicide rate, to the music 'scene' failing in its provision of models of 'acceptable behaviour' and boundaries:

> It actually does the reverse—it valorises outrageous behaviour and the acting out of aggressive, sexual and destructive impulses that most of us dare only live out in fantasy… The music industry needs to consider these findings to discover ways of recognising and assisting young musicians in distress. (Kenny, 2014a)

Substance use/abuse and the music industries are inextricably linked in a live performance context. While the *World Drug Report 2014* produced by the United Nations (2014) identified Australians as being amongst the highest users in several categories of recreational drug use *per capita*, alcohol and drug use more broadly in the popular music industries in Australia remains largely undocumented. McMillen (2014), however, provided a detailed series of interviews with several well-known contemporary Australian musicians who candidly discussed prescriptive and illegal drug use. McMillen highlighted perceived relationships between creativity and drug use, which speak to the powerful relationship that artistic creativity has with positive emotion or 'affect' (see Madden & Bloom, 2004, p. 135), and discussed the ways in which professional musicians navigated their way through and out of substance abuse (McMillen, 2014). Similarly, Dobson (2011) conducted a study on the workplace pressures and challenges faced by young musicians in the UK and identified a link between alcohol consumption and sector demands. Undeniably, substance abuse remains a significant issue in the new music industries. Substance use may range from musicians who feel tense on stage and use alcohol beforehand to relax, to high-energy performers who use amphetamines on the days they may be 'flat' or tired. There are also issues of performance anxiety to consider (for example, Papageorgi, Creech, & Welch, 2013), the potential isolation of 'being on the road', possible self-medication, and the consumption of alcohol provided by venues in relation to contractual riders.[2] A prominent example of substance abuse came to light in early 2016 when rapper 360 disclosed his addiction to over-the-counter codeine medication Nurofen Plus, consuming up to 90 tablets a day before overdosing in early 2015 (Carter, 2016). 360 subsequently released a song detailing his drug use explicitly in the song's lyrics, revealing that the overdose occurred immediately before a scheduled performance (Carter, 2016).

Additional environmental factors, particularly in relation to hearing loss and musicians (for example, Barlow, 2010), form another area of wellbeing that warrants further attention. For example, Schink, Kreutz, Busch, Pigeot and Ahrens (2014) compared the incidence of hearing loss in professional musicians with the general population in Germany and determined that professional musicians have a high risk of contracting hearing disorders. Clearly, the implementation of preventive measures aimed specifically to reduce the likelihood of hearing loss in the new music industries need to be further supported and expanded. Other significant factors, detailed below, have received little attention.

The ongoing realities of practice we identified related to contractual obligations, issues relating to health and wellbeing, fiduciary aspects of associated individuals or organisations, and the legalities of copyright and royalty collection. Of primary significance is a perceived lack, from the perspective of some of our participants, of Workplace Health and Safety (WHS) concerns in a range of musical contexts. This perception expressed by some of our participants is significant, particularly when compared to other industries, and may partly account for the physical and mental stresses documented by sector workers (van den Eynde et al., 2015). Burrows (2016) details the ongoing psychological and social toll on musicians caused by precarious employment and financial circumstances, illustrating the lack of correlation between industry success (measured in terms of live performances, critical acclaim, and sales) and actual revenue or career stability. The concept of musical success (see Hughes, Keith, Morrow, Evans, & Crowdy, 2013) may also relate to notions of 'the celebrity performer' (Smith, 2013, p. 27). Jenny Biddle (singer-songwriter) summarised several concerning issues that are, for some artists, also unfortunate realities:

> The constant rejection, or the body problems, the strain on your body or the instability of money, not having mentorship, not knowing who to turn to and the management crisis, there is just so much... it is really trial and error and you don't have a place to turn to.

The most prominent realities brought out in our study are discussed below under the following six categories: career sustainability, networking, the changing roles of live performance and recorded music, image, managing expectations and WH&S.

CAREER SUSTAINABILITY IN AN AUSTRALIAN CONTEXT

The music industries in Australia are significant in economic terms. The International Federation of the Phonographic Industry (IFPI, 2014) reports that Australia ranks sixth in the world in its total music consumption (90), while in terms of digital consumption alone, Australia ranks fifth. Of all Australian musicians, 67% are freelance or self-employed (Throsby & Zednick, 2010, p. 53) and of the remaining 33 % who work for salary or wages, it is classical musicians who are more commonly protected as employees within institutional employment structures such as symphony orchestras. The contemporary music industries, meanwhile, include many independent, casual and DIY solo artists/musicians and bands without such institutional protection (Morrow, 2006, p. 12). There also appear to be gendered constraints within the music industries (see Hesmondhalgh & Baker, 2011).

Hughes et al. (2014) identified that while the opportunities for those involved in the sector to perform, share and/or distribute their music have never been as great, the challenges to be heard and/or to sustain a consistent revenue stream from music have never been greater. As a consequence, contemporary musicians operating within the new music industries can face significant pressures in relation to both financial and emotional sustainability. Not surprisingly, career longevity and financial hardship were both identified as sector issues. The commodification of artistry and the construct of instant celebrity in relation to television talent competitions were also identified as concerns that were expressed by several participants. Our findings within an Australian context provide a parallel to Stahl's (2013) discussion of *American Idol*.

The dedicated work ethic required for career development and sustainability was highlighted by Tim Hart (singer-songwriter and member of band Boy & Bear):

> I think there are more opportunities now than there have ever been. Because it is not a matter of record companies investing into the certain few, it is about who wants it the most and are you prepared to work hard enough to take it on.

Artists put themselves on the line, in both a fiduciary and an emotional sense, in their attempts to 'have a go'. Robert Scott (Founder of Source Music Publishing and licensing and creative manager of Embassy Music Publishing and Music Sales), noted:

> I think that initially it is about survival. It is really stressing to people that if they want to do music, they have to be, not only 100%, but 110% committed [to it]. It needs to be in every fibre of their being because it is hard, it is really hard.

Little or intermittent remuneration, industry obstacles and long hours were other factors identified that impacted on career sustainability. Described by Tom Harris (Founder of White Sky Music, a specialist music business management and bookkeeping company) as 'the 30 hours or the 50 hours a week [required] to make [a music career] work', lengthy working hours were identified as the industry standard for both artist managers and related stakeholders.

Networking

The significance of networking among friends and fans was stressed by participants as being beneficial for both career development and sustainability. The link between this theme and the issue of alcoholism and drug use/abuse, however, also became evident in a way that parallels with Hesmondalgh and Baker's findings (see 2011, p. 153). They identified that in a UK context, networking regularly occurs in pubs and clubs in which there is a ready supply of substances. However, in terms of the desired outcome from such networking, Robert Scott noted:

> You can tell the people that are really going to be successful, you can tell because they are determined and they have the right people around them. They attract the right people because their sense of determination galvanises people into action.

Another participant, Fernando J. Moguel (singer-songwriter and producer) noted that networking was 'even more valuable than money' in its potential for sharing music and workload relief. Participants stressed the importance of building networks to reduce the risk of burnout due to the creative and administrative work required as a DIY artist. This was emphasised by Dr Daniel Robinson (artist and educator) who noted that sometimes career development is 'all too hard and [artists/bands] burn out because they don't have the infrastructure around them to be sustainable in their art'. In addition to helping artists avoid burnout, benefits of the positive relationships that can be built through networking were identified as being key to our participants' wellbeing. While 'building resilience' (Seligman, 2011, p. 16) is the key to wellbeing within these industries, the issue of *how* to build positive networking relationships was also stressed by one of our participants. Leanne de Souza (artist manager) highlighted the need to find an appropriate network for the individual:

> It's about seeking out the right people, the right culture, the right companies that are all actually buying into that artist for whatever reason that might be, to release singles and EPs, or recording, or touring or whatever is the right thing for them.

Participants also noted examples of emerging artists/bands making poor networking/collaborative choices. These included signing agreements too early, without appropriate advice, with inequitable percentage rights and/ or that proved not to be in the best interests of an emerging career or related image.

LIVE VERSUS RECORDED

Live performances and/or recordings were identified by participants as both opportunities and challenges, and were context dependent. The impact and scarcity of live performance venues, for example, was noted as a challenge by several participants and is often cited in the literature as being an issue confronting musicians (see Johnson & Homan, 2002; Homan et al., 2015, 2016). Traditionally, live performance has been vital to career sustainability. Currently, the necessity to perform live is often aligned to album releases. However, it can also be aligned to the type of music being performed, as Tim Hart explained:

> It has to be about connection with the people that enjoy our music... Gone are the days of the artists shrouded in mystery. For bands like us, you have got to be down to earth, stay connected, and you have got to play a lot of live shows. You know what it's like, if you go and see a great live show, you buy the record. You know you can stream it for free, but it's more than that, you want to get on board with what that artist is doing.

Less acknowledged, in relation to live music, is the impact of 'oversupply' of good musicians, which was a factor reported in relation to the live music scene in Melbourne, Australia. Helen Marcou (Co-founder of Bakehouse Studios) explained: 'There are so many musicians in this town that they are constantly under-cutting each other for gigs. Working musicians lose out when people are prepared to play for free all the time.'

Digital and online music technology offers another opportunity and challenge for recorded outputs. On the one hand, the digitisation of music enables access to DIY recording technologies and online distribution. Conversely, potential production costs are now incurred by the artist-producer, and online streaming potentially impacts the revenue stream for independent artists. Yet, despite the controversy surrounding online streaming (such as Taylor Swift removing her catalogue from Spotify), Jenny Biddle surmised its use in general:

> Digital, that could be a good thing and a bad thing. Bad for CD sales, good for fusion. I feel like there is more power to the indie musicians now.

I would have, 10 years ago, just found it really impossible, living as a muso, it's good to be able to do it.

While the digitisation of music may impact on practice realities in relation to physical sales, the significance of recording as product is highly relevant in gaining exposure for the independent artist. Robert Scott explained:

> You just don't know when that success may come. If you're really good at your art then it is going to come and you need to believe that it is going to come but it is not necessarily around the corner... You need to go and manufacture [a recording] so that you can go and sell it at all of your shows because that is revenue... it's your business card.

Tim Hart agreed with the significance of recording as product, viewing recording as an essential career investment:

> You need to be prepared to put your money where your mouth is and invest in your career. In that sense, a good sound engineer, and maybe a good producer. Every artist will have a vision of what they want themselves to sound like, so go in and pay the money and record the songs with a great engineer who can hopefully recreate the songs the way you are hearing them in your head.

IMAGE

The difficulties surrounding the construction and portrayal of image (visual, artistic, musical) was a theme that emerged in our findings. Liz Tripodi (vocal teacher, entrepreneur and performer) discussed the confronting nature of image-related comments such as, 'Your image does not fit where the industry is at the moment.' Several participants viewed a relevant image, together with image-related issues, as being vital to career viability. While managed artists may have the support of an extended network in the creation and maintenance of their individual image, the self-managed artist is largely left to his/her own perceptions. This allows artists to maintain artistic control while being able to call on appropriate expertise when and if required, as Jenny Biddle explained. Noting that her stylist did not try 'to create me into something that I am not', Biddle commented:

> I just hired a stylist actually, because image is a very unique point... [I felt that I was] not presenting what [my image] needs to be. I don't want to get lost in that though, fireworks and glamour. I don't think that's what I am about.

While several participants talked about the relevance of appropriate image or the integrity of an image, perhaps most telling in relation to the perception of image is Sinead O'Connor's open letter to Miley Cyrus. O'Connor warned:

> I am extremely concerned for you that those around you have led you to believe, or encouraged you in your own belief, that it is in any way 'cool' to be naked and licking sledgehammers in your videos. It is in fact the case that you will obscure your talent by allowing yourself to be pimped, whether it's the music business or yourself doing the pimping. (O'Connor cited in Strang, 2013)

The public nature of artists' creative work exacerbates issues relating to image, particularly with regard to perceived appropriateness or self-esteem.

Managing Expectations

The realities of practice are often aligned to the realization of expectations and the concept of success (Smith, 2013; Hughes et al., 2013; Hall, 2014). Managing expectations was identified as a recurring theme in participant perspectives. One of the reassuring aspects of artist expectations in relation to success was the notion of self-satisfaction, as Tim Hart explained:

> If it was financial then it would be a tiny, tiny percentage of musicians that were successful. But if it was aesthetic… then that conjures up images of perception. I think it has to be success that leads to self-satisfaction. That's the only thing that matters.

Versatility and adaptability were two emergent themes that resonated strongly with sustainability and correlate to our discussion in Chapter 3. Consistent with the evolutionary nature of the new industries, Talia Raso (a music business student at the time of interview and an emerging artist manager) explained that the most important skill for music industry practitioners is:

> Adaptability, because if we put our head into one scenario and think that is how it is going to be then as soon as something changes we are lost. We might be learning now and trying to get into the industry with all guns blazing on what is happening, but it won't be like this in a few years time.

Building resilience at the coalface was deemed essential for career development and longevity. Tim Hart advised that emerging artists should have:

> a thick skin. People are going to tell you that you are no good. People are going to tell you that they have heard what you are doing before. People are going to say they are not hearing a hit. You need vision. You need an idea of where you want to end up otherwise you will be aimless. And you need determination, when you feel like no one is believing in you, then you have to believe in yourself.

WORKPLACE HEALTH AND SAFETY

In the Western world, health and wellbeing of workers is a concept that underpins government legislation and policies. In Australia, 'promoting population health and wellbeing' (Australian Government, 2013, p. 1) is also a national strategic research priority. Given this emphasis, it was alarming that our research uncovered situations where the health and wellbeing of sector workers was either overlooked or compromised. Reported situations where issues relating to the health and wellbeing of sector workers included a band that continued to play at an outdoor event in torrential rain with puddles of water accumulating under instrument leads, an artist being bitten by an audience member during a performance, children playing on stage during a performance through and around what could have been heavy electrical equipment and leads, musicians consuming excess alcohol because of access to free alcohol through contractual riders, general safety in various contexts including particular venues and in some business practices, and the stress of dealing with perceived unprofessional behaviour by sector workers. For some artists, issues relating to financial viability or promoting music were paramount to health and wellbeing considerations. Jenny Biddle explained:

> There's no sick leave. I've had to weigh up whether it is worth missing a gig for fear of ruining the voice or ruining my arms. I have had to weigh it up in terms of missing a gig and my reputation… often, I put my safety and my health second so I can put on [my] music. At times, I have put it second where it gets to a point where it's either really dangerous or [difficult to] physically play.

The irregular hours of sector workers was also cited in relation to health and wellbeing. Compared with regular working hours those of music sector workers are more varied and often transient and erratic. Biddle continued: 'I have really had to learn to just accept that it's an irregular job and I don't have to fit into the mould like everyone else thinks it should be.' Such irregular hours can have an impact on such an artist's mental health when considering creative energy and the notion of the body's clock. Crabtree and Crabtree (2011) noted that: 'Creative people, particularly performers, live and work to a different rhythm than other people. This has huge implications for their body clock and how they manage their internal world' (p. 47). This issue is especially nuanced when the artist is touring internationally, particularly if they are alternating between the southern and northern hemispheres, Sydney and London for example, to perform and play tours. Crabtree and Crabtree (2011) continued:

> Stress on the body clock, or circadian rhythm, has been associated with triggering bipolar disorder... [for] performers, who have a different sleep/wake cycle, deregulation or difficulties in the internal body clock, may contribute to mood disorders—particularly depression and bipolar disorder. (p. 47)

The literature also documents other pragmatic health and safety concerns and issues in relation to sector workers. The necessity for adequate safety checks, for example, has been an ongoing concern for performing musicians. This is evident in the safety concerns underpinning the legendary Van Halen covert technical rider[3] clause (Article 126) used in the 1980s (Littlewood, 2013). A more recent example is in relation to the electrocution of Emmure singer Frankie Palmeri, who was on stage with his band in Russia in 2013 when he was electrocuted while holding his microphone (Childers, 2013). Similarly, guitarist Dominic Zyntek had both hands severely burned when he was electrocuted during a routine sound-check on the P&O *Pride of Hull* ferry in 2012 (Edmonds, 2014). Zyntek was unable to play for several months, and described the incident as 'like I was being burnt alive for a few minutes' (Zyntek cited in Edmonds, 2014). The sound-check was carried out despite the manager of Zyntek's band also being electrocuted the previous day. Compensation was awarded to Zyntek, at which time his solicitor, Sally Rissbrook, called for more diligence in relation to sector health and safety:

> Dominic was informed that it was safe to use the equipment even though a separate incident happened the previous night where Dominic's manager was taken to hospital as precaution after being electrocuted on the same stage... If the correct health and safety checks are not adhered to then incidents like this will continue to happen. (Rissbrook cited in Edmonds, 2014)

Conclusion

Of prime significance was our finding that some participants noted that there was no exercise of or adherence to the duty of care required under such legislation as the New South Wales WHS Act 2011 in a range of industry contexts. In the new music industries, there is no apprenticeship system and artists are now largely without formal support and learning networks. As such, and as our findings identify, artists may be susceptible to exploitation, manipulation and/or to being in situations in which they are taken advantage. There were real concerns raised regarding artist safety. Issues including misogyny, sexism and gender-based abuse, along with isolation, fear of the unknown and varying levels of security (personal and financial) were identified in participant experiences. Psychological issues included stress, the pressure to succeed, depression and performance anxiety; self-medication and substance abuse often followed. Physical injuries were also noted including repetitive strain injury, vocal tiredness and hearing-related concerns. Financial hardship was frequently reported, as were the limitations posed by an erratic revenue stream (for example, the preclusive cost of in-ear monitors). Although some realities encountered have always existed in popular music practices, in the twenty-first century many of the challenges may be circumvented through established preventative measures and mechanisms:

> At the very least, those who make their livings from these young people need to learn to recognise early signs of emotional distress, crisis, depression and suicidality and to put some support systems in place to provide the necessary assistance and care. (Kenny, 2014a)

The work of Support Act (2016) should be commended in this regard and awareness of such initiatives needs to increase.

Notes

1. Support Act's website stated: 'The power of music is something we all feel. So many events in life need a soundtrack: a long road trip, a first dance at a wedding, a carefully chosen piece to mark a loved one's passing. Music makes memories. And yet, as a professional, a career in music can be uncertain and risky. Even the most talented find themselves unable to work when illness, injury or some other problem strikes. Without an income, a setback can quickly become a crisis' (Support Act, 2016).

2. In this context, a rider is defined as involving the alcohol, food and other items that are provided to musicians by venues as part of their hospitality, sometimes in lieu of monetary payment.
3. The Van Halen rider is notorious for including specific and often bizarre requests for refreshments in the band's backstage area. However according to Littlewood (2013) this was a test designed to check whether the venue's management and technicians had properly read and implemented all the band's technical requirements; if their trifling rider requests were not met, this indicated that important and potentially dangerous oversights had been made regarding preparations for their stage performance.

References

Australian Government. (2013). *Strategic research priorities*. Canberra: Commonwealth of Australia.

Barlow, C. (2010). Potential hazard of hearing damage to students in undergraduate popular music courses. *Medical Problems of Performing Artists, 25*(4), 175.

Burrows, M. (2016). The long, hard road to rock'n'roll success: 'We're essentially skint'. *Guardian News and Media Limited* [Online]. Retrieved February 2, 2016, from http://www.theguardian.com/business/2016/jan/30/rocknroll-stardom-live-music-struggling-bands-slow-club-brawlers

Carter, L. (2016). Rapper 360's codeine addiction admission prompts calls for stricter regulations on over-the-counter medications. *ABC News* [Online]. Retrieved January 27, 2016, from http://www.abc.net.au/news/2016-01-11/360-rapper-becomes-face-of-codeine-addiction-calls-regulation/7080192

Childers, C. (2013). *Emmure frontman Frankie Palmeri electrocuted during performance in Moscow*. Loudwire. Retrieved March 1, 2016, from http://loudwire.com/emmure-frankie-palmeri-electrocuted/

Cloonan, M. (2011). Researching live music: Some thoughts on policy implications. *International Journal of Cultural Policy, 17*(4), 405–442.

Cloonan, M. (2014). Musicians as workers: Putting the UK musicians' union in to context. *MusiCultures, 41*(1), 10–29.

Crabtree, J., & Crabtree, J. (2011). *Living with a creative mind*. Sydney: Zebra Collective.

Csikszentmihalyi, M. (1996). *Creativity: Flow and the psychology of discovery and invention*. New York: Harper Perennial.

Dobson, M. C. (2011). Insecurity, professional sociability, and alcohol: Young freelance musicians. *Psychology of Music, 39*(2), 240–260.

Drus, M., Kozbelt, A., & Hughes, R. (2014). Creativity, psychopathology, and emotion processing: A liberal response bias for remembering negative information is associated with higher creativity. *Creativity Research Journal, 26*(3), 251–262.

Dunn, J. (2015). 'I didn't ruin Amy': Blake Fielder claims he wasn't responsible for early death of tragic singer Amy Winehouse. *Daily Mail* [Online]. Retrieved January 11, 2016, from http://www.dailymail.co.uk/news/article-3132487/I-didn-t-ruin-Amy-Drug-addict-former-husband-tragic-singer-Amy-Winehouse-claims-wasn-t-responsible-early-death.html

Edmonds, L. (2014). Guitarist who suffered horrific burns after he was ELECTROCUTED for two minutes as he sound-checked for ferry gig wins £6,400 compensation. *Daily Mail*. Retrieved June 13, 2014, from http://www.dailymail.co.uk/news/article-2557721/Guitarist-suffered...-two-minutes-sound-checked-ferry-gig-wins-6-400-compensation.html

Grönberg, R., (2010). *Comparing Finnish and British live music event health and safety culture: A perspective to the legislations and prevailing practices.* Thesis for degree programme in Music and Media Management, Jamk University of Applied Sciences.

Hall, R. (2014). The future of popular music education: What voice can education have? [Paper Presentation]. Association for Popular Music Education [APME] Conference, presentation, 20 June, 2014, University of Southern California, Los Angeles, US.

Hesmondhalgh, D., & Baker, S. (2011). *Creative labour: Media work in three cultural industries.* London: Routledge.

Homan, S., Cloonan, M., & Cattermole, J. (2015). *Popular music and cultural policy.* Abingdon, UK/New York: Routledge.

Homan, S., Cloonan, M., & Cattermole, J. (2016). *Popular music and the state: Policy notes.* London, UK/New York: Routledge.

Hughes, D., Keith, S., Morrow, G., Evans, M., & Crowdy, D. (2013). What constitutes artist success in the Australian music industries? *International Journal of Music Business Research, 2*(2), 61–80.

Hughes, D., Evans, M., Keith, S., & Morrow, G. (2014). A 'duty of care' and the professional musician/artist. In G. Carruthers (Ed.), *Proceedings of the commission for the education of the professional musician (CEPROM)* (pp. 31–41). Brazil: Belo Horizonte.

IFPI (International Federation of Phonographic Industry). (2014). *Recording industry numbers: The recorded music market in 2013.* London, UK: Deloitte.

Johnson, B., & Homan, S. (2002). *Vanishing acts: An inquiry into the state of live popular music opportunities in New South Wales.* Sydney: Australia Council and the NSW Ministry for the Arts.

Kenny, D. T. (2014a). The 27 club is a myth: 56 is the bum note for musicians. *The Conversation.* Retrieved January 9, 2016, from https://theconversation.com/the-27-club-is-a-myth-56-is-the-bum-note-for-musicians-33586

Kenny, D. T. (2014b). Stairway to hell: Life and death in the pop music industry. *The Conversation.* Retrieved January 9, 2016, from http://theconversation.com/stairway-to-hell-life-and-death-in-the-pop-music-industry-32735

Kenny, D. T. (2015). Music to die for: How genre affects popular musicians' life expectancy. *The Conversation.* Retrieved January 9, 2016, from http://theconversation.com/music-to-die-for-how-genre-affects-popular-musicians-life-expectancy-36660

Littlewood, M. (2013). *The truth about Van Halen's M&M rider – Just good operations* [uploaded August 7, 2013]. Retrieved October 14, 2013, at http://businessofsoftware.org/2013/08/the-truth-about-van-halens-mm-rider-just-good-operations/

Madden, C., & Bloom, T. (2004). Creativity, health and arts advocacy. *International Journal of Cultural Policy, 10*(2), 133–156.

McGuigan, J. (2010). Creative labour, cultural work and individualisation. *International Journal of Cultural Policy, 16*(3), 323–335.

McMillen, A. (2014). *Talking Smack: Honest Conversations about Drugs*. Queensland, Australia: University of Queensland Press.

Morrow, G. (2006). *Managerial creativity: A study of artist management practices in the Australian popular music industry*. Unpublished PhD thesis, Macquarie University, Sydney, Australia.

Oh, M. (2002). Bobby Brown arrested For drug possession, speeding. *MTV.com*. Retrieved January 10, 2016, from http://www.mtv.com/news/1458561/bobby-brown-arrested-for-drug-possession-speeding/

Papageorgi, I., Creech, A., & Welch, G. (2013). Perceived performance anxiety in advanced musicians specializing in different musical genres. *Psychology of Music, 41*, 18–41.

Resnikoff, P. (2013). 16 artists that are now speaking out against streaming… *Digital Music News*. Retrieved January 11, 2016, from http://www.digitalmusicnews.com/2013/12/02/artistspiracy/

Schink, T., Kreutz, G., Busch, V., Pigeot, I., & Ahrens, W. (2014). Incidence and relative risk of hearing disorders in professional musicians. *Occupational and Environmental Medicine, 71*, 472–476.

Seligman, M. (2011). *Flourish: A visionary new understanding of happiness and well-being*. New York: Free Press.

Simpson, S., & Munro, J. (2012). *Music business*. London, UK: Omnibus Press.

Smith, G. (2013). Seeking 'success' in popular music. *Music Education Research International, 6*, 26–37.

Stahl, M. (2013). *Unfree masters: Recording artists and the politics of work*. Durham, NC/London, UK: Duke University Press.

Strang, F. (2013). 'Don't let the music business make a prostitute of you': Sinead O'Connor's open letter to Miley Cyrus after she's inspired by her Nothing Compares 2 U video. *Daily Mail* [Online]. Retrieved January 23, 2016, from http://www.dailymail.co.uk/tvshowbiz/article-2442321/Sinead-OConnor-Miley-Cyrus-Dont-let-music-business-make-prostitute-you.html

Support Act. (2016). Retrieved February 26, 2016 from http://supportact.org.au/

Throsby, D., & Zednik, A. (2010). *Do you really expect to get paid? An economic study of professional artists in Australia*. Melbourne: Australia Council for the Arts.

United Nations. (2014). *World Drug Report 2014*. Vienna, Austria: United Nations Office on Drugs and Crime.

van den Eynde, J., Fisher, A., & Sonn, C. (2015). *Working in the Australian entertainment industry. Phase 2: Executive summary*. Melbourne, Victoria: Victoria University.

CHAPTER 6

Popular Music Education

Abstract Teaching popular music in higher education is multidimensional. This chapter considers how best to train students for sustainable career trajectories within the new music industries. To date, business education, particularly in tertiary settings, has tended to be treated in isolation from the 'music' component. This chapter will show how contemporary music education needs to reflect the convergence between the artist and 'business', and address the management of expectations. Multiple creativities underpin the integrated model for popular music education presented in this chapter. The relevance of artistry, individuality and entrepreneurship to music education is discussed. The chapter concludes with the ways in which education can address and prepare popular music students for the realities of practice that they may encounter.

Keywords Popular music education • Creativities • Student • Tertiary • Artistry • Individuality

Teaching popular music in higher education is multidimensional. While curriculum foci are typically centred on musical development in a range of theoretical and practical contexts, it is debatable whether curricular content and delivery also comprehensively cater to students wanting to pursue careers as popular musicians or performers (see Lebler, 2007, 2008; Feichas, 2010; Burnard, 2012, 2014; Gaunt & Westerlund, 2013;

Smith, 2013; Smith & Shafighian, 2014; Parkinson & Smith, 2015; Smith & Gillet, 2015). While we acknowledge that much can be learned and modelled informally in popular music (see Green, 2002), we discuss below popular music education specifically in the context of tertiary studies and preparing students for the new music industries.

The primary aim of the research that informs this chapter was to identify career trajectories within the real-world practices of the new music industries. The research identified that multiple creativities form a core component in this multi-industry landscape. We also identified health, safety and wellbeing concerns within these industries. This chapter now addresses these concerns within the scope of our research themes—the concept of individualisation in artistry and branding, and aspects of and preparation for working in the new music industries. We offer an integrated model for music education that encompasses the new music businesses and places multiple creativities at its core. This acknowledges that creativities are now key in all areas of popular music and business practices. Typically, business education has tended to be treated in isolation from the 'music' component (see Beckman, 2007; Daniel, 2010; Brindle, 2011; Bridgstock, 2012) in popular music studies and, as such, music business subjects have tended to be discrete units of study that separate the creative from the managerial.

This chapter will show how contemporary music programs need to reflect the convergence between the artist and business models/operations. It examines the changing relationship between artists and various music business intermediaries and argues that popular music education should comprehensively address notions of multiple creativities. Bilton (2010, p. 255) notes that creativity and management have been historically positioned as opposing concepts, but that they are increasingly converging in new models of cultural policy and business management. Our findings identify that the design of music curricula for the new industries also needs to reflect this convergence; our model of integrated music education encompasses this convergence.

NOTIONS OF MULTIPLE CREATIVITIES

Traditional music education models, such as those typically offered in the music conservatoire, often focus on instrumental and/or performance prowess, written notation, and score replication or interpretation. This focus is indeed different in new twenty-first century popular music practices, however, where the process of creativity is at the forefront (for example, songwriting, improvisation, looping technologies). Notions of creativity are not only evident in improvisatory traits and songwriting/composition, but they are central in levels of business acumen underpinning marketing strategies, networking, collaboration, and branding. More broadly, notions of creativity are evident in online and offline strategies (Keith, Hughes, Crowdy, Morrow, & Evans, 2014), in artistic attributes and intent, and in contemporary performance and production technologies. An integrated music education model that places creativity at its core finds its basis within a broader creative industries discourse. When discussing the creative industries and tertiary education, Bridgstock (2012) noted:

> While the majority of creative, performing and literary artists are self-employed, relatively few tertiary arts schools attempt to develop capabilities for venture creation and management (and entrepreneurship more broadly) and still fewer do so effectively. (p. 122)

Bridgstock addresses the underlying conceptual and philosophical issues encountered by arts educators and argues that while entrepreneurship is essential to career success in the arts, the practice of arts-related entrepreneurship is significantly different from the practice of entrepreneurship in other businesses. With this in mind, this chapter outlines artistry and what is unique about the practice of entrepreneurship in arts practices (particularly in the new music businesses), and suggests strategies for nurturing music business entrepreneurship within tertiary popular music programs.

Arts Entrepreneurship

Bridgstock (2012) highlights that entrepreneurship in tertiary arts education should focus on 'the application, sharing or distribution of art, as well as [on] its creation or making' (p. 123). Others, such as Hausmann (2010), argue that many freelancers in the arts 'are faced with work and income insecurity while also experiencing difficulties with their self-image and self-perception as entrepreneurs' (p. 17) (see also Chapter 3). These arguments imply that career sustainability, or even initial startup development, may be impacted by lack of effective arts entrepreneurship education. Such arguments can be located within a body of literature that links creative work with economic growth in advanced economies (for example, Florida, 2011; Mellander, Florida, & Rentfrow, 2012; Gabe, Florida, & Mellander, 2013).

However, in contrast to this body of work, there is literature that suggests artists have a role to play in challenging social norms (for example, Carey, 2005) and that culture and commerce have entered an awkward alliance (for example, McGuigan, 2009a, 2009b, 2010). Following these arguments, therefore, arts entrepreneurship education may be making universities (even more) subservient to the market fundamentalism of the neoliberal agenda. As McGuigan (2010) argues:

> [I]ndividualisation addresses the paradoxical character of work and everyday life today, freer in some sense yet also harsh and isolating. It is especially pronounced in the 'creative industries' enabling a tantalizing sense of expressivity at the cost of exceptional difficulties in working life—including insecurity, poor pay and conditions. (p. 334)

Within the context of potential and 'exceptional difficulties in working life' (McGuigan, 2010, p. 334), and in light of our findings on the realities of practice, the ability of tertiary students to be 'employable'[1] and to maintain sustainable income stream/s while being adaptable and/or versatile is more complex than preparing for a specific vocation. The argument informing this chapter is that knowledge about how to facilitate group creativity/creativities, and how to locate oneself within a context from which distributed, and collaboratively emergent ideas can arise, is key to career longevity. Furthermore, educators have a moral imperative (Beckman, 2007, p. 93) to use their own creativities to design programs of study that are suited to the nature of the industries into which our students graduate, as highly networked improvisational groups are the norm within the new music industries (Sawyer & DeZutter, 2009).

A primary issue for the field of the new music industries in Australia relates to the statistic that four in five professional artists maintain their own businesses (Throsby & Zednik, 2011).[2] In an international context, the incidence of artists self-employed is also high, as was noted in Bridgstock (2012, p. 122). Given this incidence, accountable education must involve teaching arts entrepreneurship for those students undertaking tertiary music education. There is also an implication here for students to work towards setting up their own businesses before they graduate. In a case study of similar issues in the United Kingdom, Smith (2013) noted that, 'a pedagogy for employability should aim to instil in students the skills for, and a sense of, collaborative entrepreneurialism, because it is widely agreed that a key to achievement in the professional music environment of the future is likely to be an ability to work successfully in teams' (p. 193). This reality of practice for students within the new music industries exists whether or not popular music educators put a determinate commitment towards employability at the core of their learning and teaching strategies; however, it would be an expectation that student graduate capabilities reflect the industries in which they aim to work.

The career models and realities of practice identified in our research are particularly pertinent given that the democratisation of technologies has facilitated individualisation in the DIY music economy and that the realities of practice are complex. Overwhelmingly, our analysis of career development within the new music industries identified that the artist is increasingly becoming either DIY or an entrepreneur. In both scenarios, artists are free to explore business opportunities or to establish their music as a business. Perhaps musicians have traditionally been 'artist-entrepreneurs', treating their music as a business in that companies were often established (albeit by third parties) to manage all of the income streams stemming from their work. As was discussed in Chapter 2, however, labels may now devolve the risks pertaining to record production onto artists and their managers, leading artists to take on more risks themselves. Under the Entrepreneur model, record labels may increasingly proceed with 'risk-free gusto' by focusing their efforts on the marketing and distribution of recordings. In this scenario, all of the financial risk involved with producing the recordings is externalized by the record label and becomes the responsibility of the artist. This in itself suggests that the artists need to be grounded in business acumen and strategies, while being creative in their ability to produce output and image that enables them to stand out in the crowd and receive due artistic and financial rewards.

Team Creativity

In the DIY economy, the onus is on the artist to initiate, coordinate and manage more aspects of their 'craft'. Because the artist has to build and coordinate their own team, an understanding of team creativity theory is useful. In this context, it is problematic to separate music education from music business education. By positioning management and artistic creativity as opposing forces, creativity may be hindered. Both musical creativity and managerial creativity/entrepreneurship involve manipulating and exploiting ideas, and intrinsic motivation is key in both (Bilton, 2010).

However, while it is easy to posit the argument that artists are intrinsically motivated to create music, it is harder to argue that artist managers (and in the new industries, DIY artist management) are also intrinsically motivated (Csikszentmihalyi, 1996, p. 110). This is because 'management' is more commonly associated with extrinsic motivators such as financial reward. However, when the artist and the manager are the same entity, this divide is subsumed. Even if an artist is self-managed or engages a manager, a team typically builds around the artist. An understanding of the role of interpersonal interaction and teams is therefore crucial.

Reality Checks

In addition to education in the fields of musical creativities and managerial creativity/entrepreneurship, students also need to be educated as to the realities of practice they may face. The previous chapter detailed the realities of practice often encountered in the new music industries. Such practice realities may impede the wellbeing (physical and/or mental) and career sustainability of artists. In addition to identifying contributing factors that may negatively impact on the wellbeing of artists, an integrated music education model needs to prepare students in ways that ensure that:

> every individual realizes his or her own potential, can cope with the normal stresses of life, can work productively and fruitfully, and is able to make a contribution to her or his community. (World Health Organisation, 2014)

As outlined in our integrated model below, an understanding of the realities of practice is integral to the mental and physical wellbeing of artists.

EMERGENT THEMES

The following themes were identified in the analyses of our focus group and interview data.[3] They are significant; each informs the development on the integrated music education model. Participant quotes are included where relevant to the themes.

Theme 1: Artist-Entrepreneur

Rather than the artist-entrepreneur being a force of disruptive 'creative destruction' (Schumpeter, 1939), the value placed on this form of entrepreneurship reflects the increased workload that has been placed on artists themselves, as was detailed in Chapters 2, 3 and 5. Participants spoke of the creative strategies that come into play through self-management. This was particularly evident in the ways they used social media. They also talked about financial management, merchandise, image and branding, and music dissemination. They discussed being time-poor and the need for time management strategies. Within the new music industries, the functions of artist management/self-management/artist-entrepreneur are being reconceptualised. As Robert Scott (Founder of Source Music Publishing and Licensing and Creative Manager, Embassy Music Publishing Music Sales) surmised with regard to pursuing a career in music: 'It's about looking for opportunity, I don't know how you encourage that but I think that music is a degree in entrepreneurialism.' Tom Harris (Founder of White Sky Music, a specialist music business management and bookkeeping company) noted the changing emphasis in desired revenue stream options: 'Once upon a time, giving your song to a TV commercial was a bad thing and there was a backlash. Now, you get high-fived, everyone wants to do it, it is gold to have your music in an ad.'

In addition, in a keynote presentation at leading Australian music industry conference BIGSOUND, artist manager John Watson (2013) noted:

> [T]he majority of artists now are having to bring a lot more innovation into their career, and that's a good thing. And the pace of change is huge... [it's] moving really fast and so you have to be mindful of that.

In relation to the notion of change and the DIY economy, Joe Vesayaporn (global sales director of Music Glue) noted:

> What people are expecting has changed. I meet far less people who are idealistic and think that they just want to get a record deal and that will solve all of their problems and let someone else take care of everything else for me. That has been happening less and less.

Theme 2: Shared Creativity

The increased use of the term 'artist-entrepreneur(ship)' has in part been caused by the breakdown of the conceptual divide between management and creativity. In terms of research, this shift is accompanied by an examination of team-level creative synergy, in which creative ideas, instead of being generated by one mind, are generated by groups (Kurtzberg & Amabile, 2000). A common theme emerging from the focus groups was that artists themselves need to increase their knowledge of management and that if they aim to be professional musicians, they will need, at some stage, to build a broader 'creative' team around them.

In discussing a business entitled 'I Manage My Own Music' (Cloher, 2013), which involves running workshops for self-managed artists, Tom Harris explained artist-entrepreneurship in the following way:

> I think that is great, preparing artists and helping them with where they want to go is really important. I do think that ultimately for long-term career success, that kind of thing is good for the early days, but to be an actual career musician or artist, you need to have the team in place. If we're talking about artist development then I don't think that the best thing is for them to be spending 20 hours a week mucking around on social media or spending hours dealing with booking agents.

Shared creativity was also seen in the mentoring role of industry representatives by Clare Cottone (artist):

> Even though I am self-managed, I have a couple of successful music managers giving me some really good advice. So with their guidance I am doing this album release differently to how I did the last one.

Involving industry representatives in an educative and informative way was seen by Lauren Porter (artist) as aiding creative practice:

> I did the 'I Manage My Own Music' [IMMM] course last year... It's difficult sometimes as an independent musician to even know where to start when you are putting out your first records, but IMMM really helped! They bring different speakers in and you can ask them anything in a really supportive environment. You leave feeling so much more knowledgeable and confident!

While discussing the team-building process in which a self-managed artist engages, Helen Marcou (Co-founder of Bakehouse Studios) noted:

> By the same token, there's a point to it, like anything, it is a micro business, there's a point where you take on a bookkeeper, you take on an accountant and often from Jen Cloher's advice you surround yourself with the people you need at that point in your business.

Discussing multiple creativities, Watson (2013) also noted:

> The big opportunity and challenge for artists and those around them, is that artists now have to redefine, more broadly, what it means to be a creative human being, and so do all the people around them.

Theme 3: Securing Additional Funding

Self-managed artist-entrepreneurs still need financial resources, and within the context of a discussion of the rise of the culture of participation (Collins & Young, 2010), participants raised the issue of when best to secure government funding to support a self-managed artist-entrepreneur. Participants identified that government funding (and support) is highly competitive alongside the suggestion there will never be enough funding opportunities to service the demand. An up-to-date knowledge of available funding from state, federal, and even philanthropic sources, together with grant application writing skills, are therefore important in ensuring a stable career for the contemporary musician. Kevin Weaver (artist) stated that being more informed about grant opportunities would help in career development and other opportunities:

> [G]overnment grants, that has been spoken about more, knowing more about how they work and what we can get from that and how we can provide a benefit for them to see why they would give us a grant, what's the criteria around that. That could help in going overseas as well.

There are initiatives and funding opportunities to assist artists in showcasing overseas; Sounds Australia was designed as a specific initiative established 'to provide a cohesive and strategic platform to assist the Australian music industry to access international business opportunities' (Sounds Australia, 2016).

Theme 4: Externalising Financial Risk

Larger entities in the music business are externalising financial risk by making asset generation and accounting for marketing spend the artist's responsibility. Artists therefore need to be educated regarding how to manage such risk. An interesting juxtaposition emerged from our focus groups, with some participants explaining that they believed the industry to be constituted by many more 'small and nimble' entities than in the past, while others noted that there has been increased monopolisation. We interpret this contradiction as we expressed in Chapter 2, in that while many smaller players can establish sustainable businesses in the music industries, there are also a number of very large entities that generate revenue from the aggregate of the many smaller entities or artists and convergent music education needs to reflect this. Whether artists are dealing with small or large entities, they need to develop a range of business and communication skills so as to successfully navigate their own pathway. This has implications for music education to include a range of career models, business strategies and practices in course content.

Theme 5: Openness and Divergent Thinking

Due to the difficulties involved in building and sustaining a musical career (Hughes, Keith, Morrow, Evans, & Crowdy, 2013a, 2013b), it is important that students are educated to embrace openness and creative thinking. Openness and creative or divergent thinking are needed because, as Hughes et al. (2013a, 2013b) noted, there is no single model for career development in the music industries. As Joe Vesayaporn also noted:

> I would say that there is no set right or wrong, you can pick and choose what you need. Whether you're successful or not is a side issue… I think you can definitely choose to go different ways and I would even say that is on a global scale. You could be doing something incredibly traditional in Australia, but as new markets open up elsewhere you could choose to try and do things differently because they are new markets and you are going in separately.

In addition, there is a strong connection between openness and divergent thinking and the continuous innovation that is needed:

> The challenge now is… to keep finding new ways to fascinate, new ways to be remarkable; not just that song, but the next song, and the next song and the one after it, and the next album after that and the next tour after that (Watson, 2013).

An Integrated Music Education Model

The emergent themes identify that the demand for research-led integrated music education is timely. This is because accessibility in and to the music industries has never been so great. The contemporary music industries now present a range of opportunities for emerging artists to share, showcase and develop their music. Alongside the myriad of opportunities are the complex challenges which artists and musicians must face. Undeniably, it is the role of education to address the challenges posed by the increased responsibilities and opportunities. Music education therefore needs to facilitate comprehensive understanding of the new industries. Furthermore, it needs to encompass the creative core evident in the emergent themes of artist-entrepreneurship, shared creativity (for example, team-building), securing additional funding (for example, procuring funding), externalising financial risk (for example, risk factors) and openness and divergent thinking (for example, reflexivity; offline/online strategies).

The integrated model we propose (see Fig. 6.1) converges the three main components of artistry, individuality and entrepreneurship.

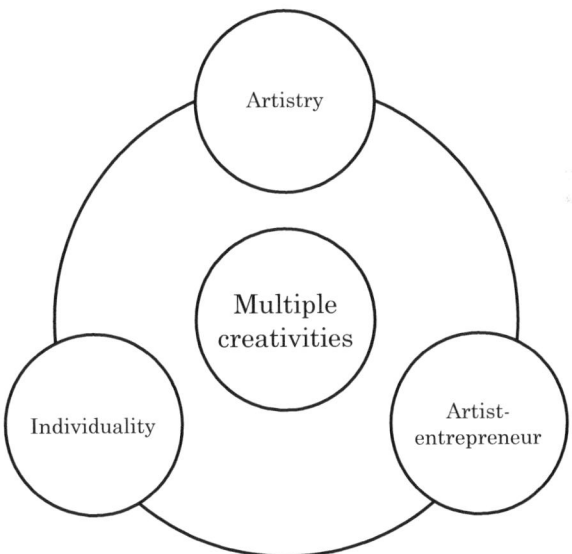

Fig. 6.1 An integrated music education model

Artistry

Contemporary artistry involves more than the traditional concepts of instrumental capability and performance (see Hughes, 2010, 2014). It now encompasses the use of technologies and innovative music production techniques. Our findings identify that it is no longer sufficient to confine music education to the development of a specific ability. Rather, contemporary music education needs to address the complexities of artistry and the creativity that underpins contemporary musicality in the ways outlined in Chapter 4. Creative interpretation, creative outputs and creative production aesthetics are prized artistic traits. While popular music has a tradition of continuous evolution, production technologies are also constantly evolving. This has implications for all artists in relation to their resultant aesthetic. Preventative strategies in relation to injuries in instrumental or context specific situations (for example, hearing loss; vocal damage), as were outlined in Chapter 5, should also be included. Education needs to facilitate a comprehensive view of artistry that accounts for these traits in ways that effectively focus on and communicate artistry. In Fig. 6.2, artistry in education is situated within an awareness of career opportunities and the field. The multifaceted components that underpin artistry are also identified.

Individuality

Participants were unanimous in the view that while the opportunities for involvement in the new music industries have never been so great, as was outlined in Chapter 3, the challenge of the ability to be seen or heard in the new digital economy is often difficult. More competition (both offline and online), engagement in social media and the significance of the 'song' were all cited as challenges that impacted on the realised level of artistic exposure. The emphasis on the 'song', rather than on an album per se, was viewed as crucial for artist exposure and subsequent interest; as Tim Hart noted, 'It has to be about the song. We have nothing else. What are you going to look forward to? I need to have that song, I wonder what else they have?' The need for individuality (used here to encompass both the solo artist and the collective such as a 'distinctive' band) was also evident in the participant focus on the development of individualisation, clear artistic intent and the facility for artists to be identifiable. This included the development of distinctive musical/vocal sound; more significantly though, it was apparent in the context of developing a specific individual image and

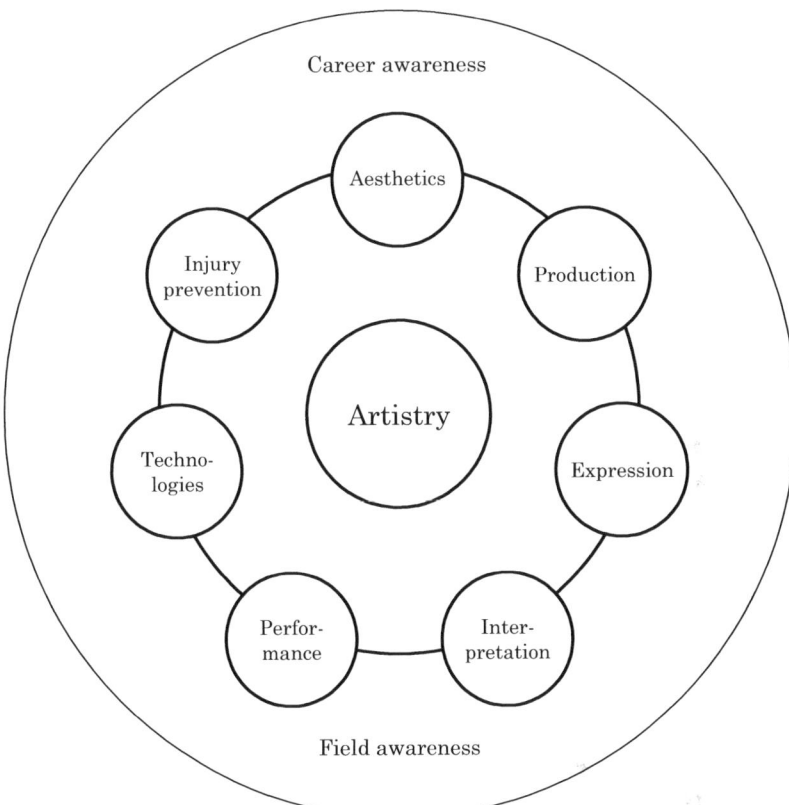

Fig. 6.2 Artistry component

brand that was consistent through various artistic components such as the musical, the visual and the technological. This facility for individualisation was clearly underpinned by multiple creativities and also encompassed the interpersonal or collaborative skills required to realise those creativities.

Reflection was also viewed as being a critical skill that aided individualisation. Participants noted that analysis of or reflection on career approaches including strategies (business and artistic), performances and recordings provided learning opportunities. Opportunities for individual reflection and reflexivity should therefore be facilitated in music education.

As this component focuses on individuality and is also situated within career opportunities and the field (see Fig. 6.3), it should also focus on

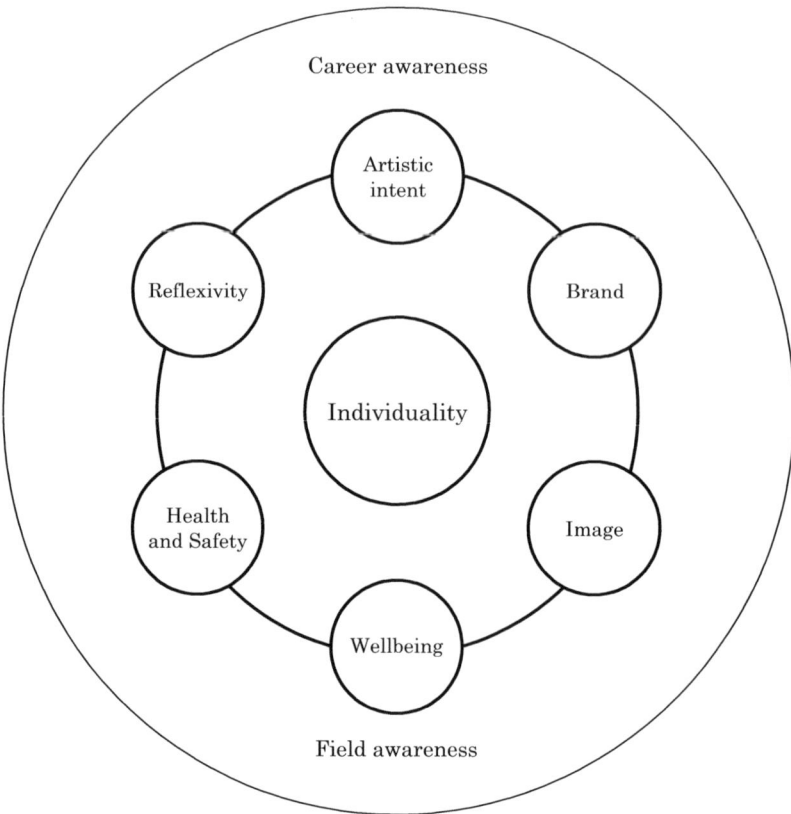

Fig. 6.3 Individualisation component

aspects of health and wellbeing. For example, it would seem imperative to have a focus on vocal demands and singing in popular music given the high incidence of singers who have suffered either vocal injuries or vocal health issues (see Hughes, 2013). It should include the development of strategies to deal with the potential impact on lifestyle (for example, substance abuse; anxiety). This includes securing adequate insurance coverage; Christopher Chow (industry lawyer) noted:

> Many artists now have all sorts of insurance. They are cottoning on to the fact that there is a risk they might not be able to perform and travel forever,

as they may get nodules in their throat, or arthritis in their hands, or perhaps just slip over and injure themselves one day. With greater understanding and education regarding these risks, comes the realisation of the requirement to protect against them.

Artist-entrepreneur

Our research clearly identifies that notions of creativity are rapidly changing. While artists now have to be artistically creative, they also need to be managerially creative. There are now significant challenges to creative outputs in relation to copyright, copyright regulation and associated artist revenue streams; there are also challenges in financial management. The facility to manage both online and offline artistic components are also formidable. In addition, workplace health and safety issues (WH & S) should be addressed.

Through an engagement with team-creativity theory, a number of strategies for nurturing music business entrepreneurship within an integrated music education model can be developed. First, because the personality traits that can be best used to predict managerial creativity are openness (or being open-minded) and the ability to think in a divergent way (Scratchley & Hakstian, 2001, p. 380), the mindset that involves positioning management and creativity as opposing concepts needs to be abandoned; a convergent approach allows for open-mindedness and divergent thinking. Underpinning this approach is a convergent transfer of information. An example of this could be to teach songwriting and production in conjunction with music business entrepreneurship. This would enable students to engage beyond the musical output and explore how their outputs could reach their target audiences. As our research findings identify, such a convergent strategy is more reflective of contemporary practices, whereby the artist-entrepreneur works across multiple areas and in multiple roles. It would also enable the management role, the artistically creative role and other required roles to coexist within units of education with the aim of facilitating the heterogeneity that is required for team creativity. These elements are illustrated in Fig. 6.4. They are also situated within career opportunities and the field. In addition to the personal insurance noted in the section above, it is relevant for the artist-entrepreneur to investigate a range of business-related insurance options (for example, securing public liability insurance in relation to the hiring of specific venues).

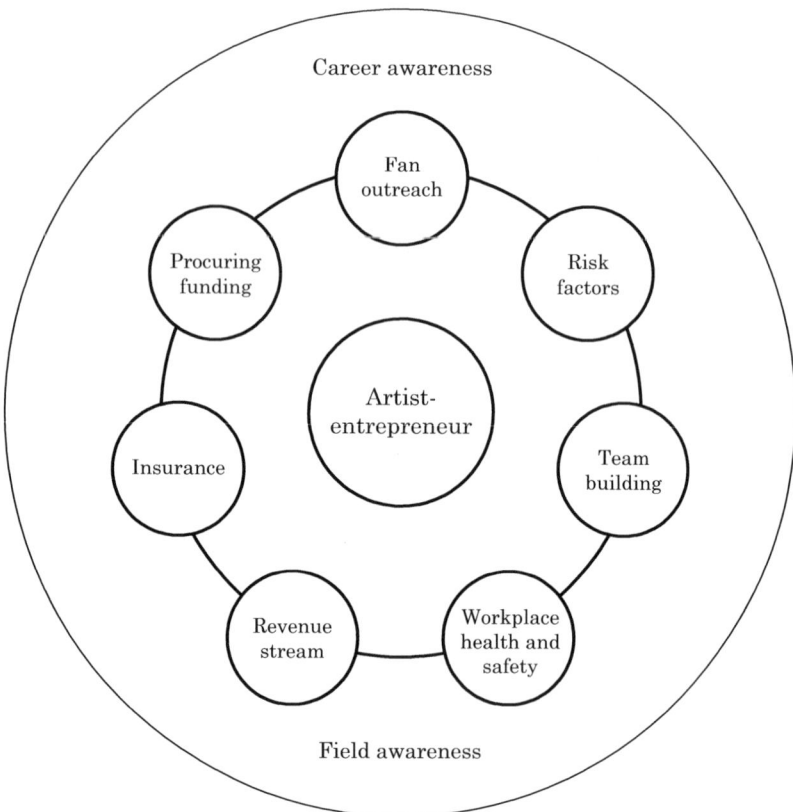

Fig. 6.4 Artist-entrepreneur component

Conclusion

This chapter has examined the research question, 'How does music education have relevancy in the contemporary multi-industry musical landscape?' Subsidiary to this primary question is whether the music business is suited to musicians, business people or both. Our analysis of career development within the contemporary music industries provided earlier in this volume suggests that a perception of tension between creativity and management dissipates when the artist becomes a self-managed artist-entrepreneur.

The call for an integrated model in music education is also indicated in other recent research findings. For example, in the *Victorian Live Music Census 2012* (Music Victoria and the City of Melbourne, 2012), of the

258 participants, 92% were self-managed and 48% of those 'rate their music industry knowledge as "Below Average" or "Poor"' (p. 55). This clearly identifies a need for education to include the multi-industry landscape or contexts (Hughes et al., 2013b) in which contemporary performances occur or through which music is now accessed and heard. As Robert Scott summarised:

> [A]rtists can take control of their career more than ever in this era, they can self-release, they can do individual deals with certain territories, they just need to have the wherewithal and the time and the education and the skills to be able to do that.

An integrated education model must also address the realities of real-world practices that can be both confronting and challenging. These realities include contractual obligations, issues relating to health and wellbeing, insurances (for example, public liability; accident cover for specific impairment), potential exploitation, fiduciary aspects of associated individuals or organisations and the legalities of copyright and royalty collection (for example, live performance royalty returns). Such realities can prove extremely challenging for some and, for others, can lead to issues of health, safety and wellbeing. Contemporary music education can address these realities in ways that best prepare students for the multiple, disrupted industries they will encounter.

NOTES

1. We are using this term in the context of sustainable income, not in relation to an 'employer' *per se*.
2. We have included this statistic here although we acknowledge that it would possibly fluctuate (higher and lower) over time.
3. The primary aim of the research that informs this chapter was to identify career trajectories within the new 'music industries' (Williamson & Cloonan, 2007). This was contextualised earlier in this volume. The research design specifically aimed at documenting the individual voice and the realities of practice through focus groups and interviews. The findings in this chapter were identified from a range of music professionals (for example, artists, artist managers, government agency representatives). A constant comparative analysis (Merriam, 1998) was utilised in the formulation of this chapter's emergent themes.

References

Beckman, G. (2007). "Adventuring" arts entrepreneurship curricula in higher education: An examination of present efforts, obstacles, and best practices. *The Journal of Arts Management, Law, and Society, 37*(2), 87–112. doi:10.3200/jaml.37.2.87-112.

Bilton, C. (2010). Manageable creativity. *International Journal of Cultural Policy, 16*(3), 255–269.

Bridgstock, R. (2012). Not a dirty word: Arts entrepreneurship and higher education. *Arts and Humanities in Higher Education, 12*(2–3), 122–137. doi:10.1177/1474022212465725.

Brindle, M. (2011). Careers and internships in arts management. In M. Brindle & C. DeVereaux (Eds.), *The arts management handbook: New directions for students and practitioners* (pp. 185–216). New York: M.E. Sharpe.

Burnard, P. (2012). *Musical creativities in practice*. Oxford: Oxford University Press.

Burnard, P. (2014). *Developing creativities in higher music education* (Kindle for Mac version). Retrieved from Amazon.com.

Carey, J. (2005). *What good are the arts?* London, UK: Faber and Faber.

Cloher, J. (2013). *The top ten things I learnt (from you) in 2013 about being a self managed indie*. Retrieved December 11, 2014, from http://imanagemymusic.com/tag/jen-cloher/

Collins, S., & Young, S. (2010). A view from the trenches of music 2.0. *Popular Music and Society, 33*(3), 339–355.

Csikszentmihalyi, M. (1996). *Creativity: Flow and the psychology of discovery and invention*. New York: Harper Perennial.

Daniel, R. (2010). Career development and creative arts students: An investigation into the effectiveness of career theory and WIL experiences on practice. *Australian Journal of Career Development, 19*(2), 14–22.

Feichas, H. (2010). Bridging the gap: Informal learning practices as a pedagogy of integration. *British Journal of Music Education, 27*(1), 47–58.

Florida, R. (2011). *The rise of the creative class revisited*. New York: Basic Books.

Gabe, T., Florida, R., & Mellander, C. (2013). The creative class and the crisis. *Cambridge Journal of Regions Economy and Society, 6*, 7–53.

Gaunt, H., & Westerlund, H. (Eds.). (2013). *Collaboration in higher music education* (Kindle for Mac version). Retrieved from Amazon.com.

Green, L. (2002). *How popular musicians learn: A way ahead for music education*. Aldershot, UK/Burlington, USA: Ashgate Publishing Limited.

Hausmann, A. (2010). German artists between Bohemian idealism and entrepreneurial dynamics: Reflections on cultural entrepreneurship and the need for start-up management. *International Journal of Arts Management, 12*(2), 17–29.

Hughes, D. (2010). Developing vocal artistry in popular culture musics. In S. Harrison (Ed.), *Perspectives on teaching singing* (pp. 244–258). Queensland, Australia: Australian Academic Press.
Hughes, D. (2013). 'OK, great sound, what are you experiencing as you're singing that?' Facilitating or interrupting the flow of vocal artistry. In O. Wilson & S. Attfield (Eds.), *Shifting sounds: musical flow. A collection of papers from the 2012 IASPM Australia/New Zealand conference*, December 5–7, Hobart, Australia, 80–87.
Hughes, D. (2014). Contemporary vocal artistry in popular culture musics: Perceptions, observations and lived experiences. In S. Harrison & O'Bryan J. (Eds.), *Teaching singing in the 21st century* (pp. 287–302). Dordrecht/Heidelberg/New York/London: Springer.
Hughes, D., Keith, S., Morrow, G., Evans, M., & Crowdy, D. (2013a). What constitutes artist success in the Australian music industries? *International Journal of Music Business Research (IJMBR), 2*(2), 60–80.
Hughes, D., Keith, S., Morrow, G., Evans, M., & Crowdy, D. (2013b). Music education and the contemporary, multi-industry landscape. In *Redefining the musical landscape: Inspired learning and innovation in music education XIX ASME National Conference Proceedings* (pp. 94–100). Brisbane, Australia.
Keith, S., Hughes, D., Crowdy, D., Morrow, G., & Evans, M. (2014). Offline and online: liveness in the Australian music industries. In V. Sarafian and R. Findlay (Eds.). *Civilisations: The State of the Music Industries, 13*, 221–241.
Kurtzberg, T., & Amabile, T. (2000). From Guilford to creative synergy: Opening the black box of team-level creativity. *Creativity Research Journal, 13*(3–4), 285–294.
Lebler, D. (2007). Student as master? Reflections on a learning innovation in popular music pedagogy. *International Journal of Music Education, 25*(30), 205–221.
Lebler, D. (2008). Popular music pedagogy: Peer learning in practice. *Music Education Research, 10*(2), 193–213.
McGuigan, J. (2009a). Doing a Florida thing: The creative class thesis and cultural policy. *International Journal of Cultural Policy, 15*(3), 291–300.
McGuigan, J. (2009b). *Cool capitalism*. London, UK: Pluto.
McGuigan, J. (2010). Creative labour, cultural work and individualisation. *International Journal of Cultural Policy, 16*(3), 323–335.
Mellandera, C., Florida, R., & Rentfrow, J. (2012). The creative class, post-industrialism and the happiness of nations. *Cambridge Journal of Regions, Economy and Society, 5*(1), 31–43.
Merriam, S. (1998). *Qualitative research and case study applications in education*. San Francisco, CA: Jossey-Bass Publishers.
Music Victoria and the City of Melbourne. (2012). *Victorian live music census 2012*. Retrieved July 16, 2013, from http://www.musicvictoria.com.au/assets/Documents/Victorian_Live_Music_Census_2012.pdf

Parkinson, T., & Smith, G. (2015). Towards an epistemology of authenticity in higher popular music education. *Action, Criticism, and Theory for Music Education, 14*(1), 93–127.

Sawyer, K., & DeZutter, S. (2009). Distributed creativity: How collective creations emerge from collaboration. *Psychology of Aesthetics, Creativity, and the Arts, 3*(2), 81–92.

Schumpeter, J. (1939). *Business cycles: A theoretical, historical, and statistical analysis of the capitalist process*. New York: McGraw Hill.

Scratchley, L., & Hakstian, R. (2001). The measurement and prediction of managerial creativity. *Creativity Research Journal, 13*(3–4), 367–384.

Smith, G. (2013). Pedagogy for employability in a Foundation Degree (Fd.A.) in creative musicianship: Introducing peer collaboration. In H. Gaunt & H. Westerlund (Eds.), *Collaborative learning in higher music education*. Farnham, UK: Ashgate.

Smith, G., & Gillet, A. (2015). Creativities, innovation, and networks in garage punk rock: A case study of the eruptörs. *Artivate: A Journal of Entrepreneurship in the Arts, 4*(1), 9–24.

Smith, G., & Shafighian, A. (2014). Creative space and the 'silent power of traditions' in popular music performance education. In P. Burnard (Ed.), *Developing creativities in higher music education: International perspectives and practices* (pp. 256–267). London, UK: Routledge.

Sounds Australia. (2016). About. *Sounds Australia*. Retrieved December 16, 2015, from http://soundsaustralia.com.au/index.php/about/

Throsby, D., & Zednik, A. (2011). Multiple job-holding and artistic careers: Some empirical evidence. *Cultural Trends, 20*(1), 9–24.

Watson, J. (2013). *Keynote Q & A with John Watson*. Interviewed by N. Megel on 12 September 2013, *BigSound*, The Judith Wright Centre, Brisbane, Australia.

Williamson, J., & Cloonan, M. (2007). Rethinking the music industry. *Popular Music, 26*(2), 305–322.

World Health Organisation. (2014). *Mental health: A state of well-being*. Retrieved December 7, 2014, from http://www.who.int/features/factfiles/mental_health/en/

CHAPTER 7

Conclusion: The 'New' Artist

Abstract This chapter outlines possible futures for the music industries in light of what is determined as the 'new' artist. Cumulative research findings, the implications of those findings, and a 'new' artist definition and model are presented which raise considerations for future musical creativities and directions. The cumulative findings also raise considerations for policy-makers, education and advocacy. The chapter concludes with consideration for musical and artistic engagement that leads well beyond disruption.

Keywords Technology • Education • Discovery • Advocacy

This concluding chapter brings together the essential elements required for the 'new artist'. Based on our ethnographic research, we highlight those skills and proficiencies that will be necessary for artists to thrive in the digital industries. While some aspects will be the responsibility of the artist themselves, we also consider the broader infrastructure required to develop artists in the new musical industries. This chapter considers the educational, technological and financial imperatives for new artists, and ultimately highlights the exciting discoveries that can be made.

Defining the 'New' Artist

In order to outline what we determine as the 'new' artist, it is useful to engage with the artist-versus-business debate, and to link this debate to an argument concerning the multiple creative self-efficacies (Bandura, 1997) or creative confidence(s) (Kelley & Kelley, 2013). We have outlined, in the preceding chapters, the models, creativities and learning that the 'new' artist engages in when navigating their chosen pathway within the new music industries. Regarding the role of the artist manager within the traditional record-label-centric music industry, Welch (2003) noted:

> Being a manager is probably the worst job, because you are the bridge between the art and the commerce and you're never going to get into a situation where you are keeping both sides happy. That's impossible. (p. 236)

Embedded here is the assumption that the artistically creative side and the business side of the music industries are not easily reconciled. In relation to the career models showcased in this book, however, it is necessary that the new artist be defined as someone who possesses precisely the multiple creativities necessary for straddling the two sides. This is because the circular model for career development and sustainability typically begins with the direct artist-to-fan relationship. In order to further understand the ways the new artist differs from the artist as previously understood, the following quote is useful:

> The idea of a conflict between creativity and commerce has also been used to illustrate the power of the music industry and has also informed numerous everyday claims about how musicians 'sell out' to the system. On one side are the heroes—the musicians, producers and performers (the creative artists); opposing them are the villains—record companies and entertainment corporations (the commercial corruptors and manipulators). (Negus, 1996, p. 46)

This rigid binary illustrated here was more appropriate when artists had to follow the linear career development process (see Fig. 2.5, Chapter 2). However, in the new music business environment, artists themselves need to develop the confidence to not only address any tensions between the artistic and the money-making aspects of music, but to find ways in which 'the generation of economic and cultural value might be harmonized such that they become complementary rather than competitive' (Throsby,

2002, p. 1). Our argument here is that for the 'new artist' to be able to do this involves multiple creative self-efficacies. As outlined in Chapter 5, self-efficacy (Bandura, 1997) is the confidence one has in their ability to achieve a certain goal, or in terms of the realities of practice, the belief and commitment to task/s that one has to get through a difficult time. Building such self-efficacy and resilience is necessary for the new artist's attempts to manage the various stresses to which they may be subject in the new music industries. Similarly, creative self-efficacy, or creative confidence (Kelley & Kelley, 2013), is required and takes a number of forms including soft to hard forms of artistic creativity as well as business-related creativities.

The model below (Fig. 7.1) represents our findings on the 'new' artist, including artist capabilities and methods of engagement. In this model, we expand on the circular model (see Fig. 2.5, Chapter 2) and orientate the methods of engagement identified in our research. For example, while evidence of a fan-to-artist relationship may be the catalyst for support, interest and reward from the music industries, artists are also free to draw on industries *in* and *for* their creative endeavours. The arrows therefore

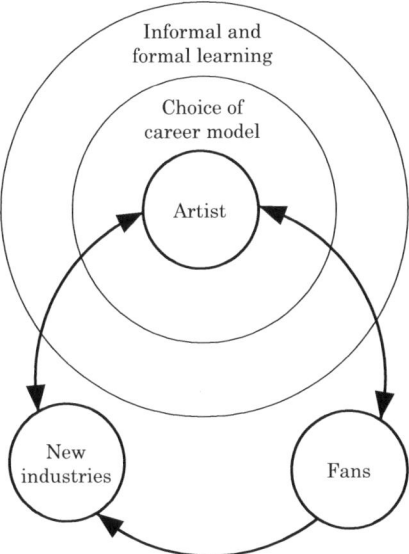

Fig. 7.1 The new artist and engagement reciprocity

represent possible engagement from multiple directions/stimuli and, as such, highlight engagement reciprocity. We also highlight that the new artist is free to choose one or more career models (360, Entrepreneur, DIY), including the potential artist-management-label 'hub' variations outlined at the end of Chapter 2. These 'hub' variations are underpinned by individual informal and formal learning as outlined in the previous chapter. The evolution of the new artist is crucial to the new industries, and while fans are not a new phenomenon, their potential impact on artist exposure and success is now immediately visible and verifiable.

Skills and Aptitudes for the 'New' Artist

The new artist in today's music climate possesses a variety of skills. Of course, artists have always tended to possess skills beyond musical ability, including basic business acumen, self-promotion and so on. However, the significant disruptions of recent years—namely, the diminishing role of major labels, the changing live performance climate, and the advent of digitisation and the Internet—have meant that artists have needed to develop new skills in response to these changes. Of course a skill base may not be commensurate with an artist's aptitude or timeframe to fulfil a particular task or role. Skill development therefore also needs to address the prioritising of roles and functions, together with strategies for devolving these to others as appropriate.

One notable characteristic of the skills required by new artists is that they are more transferable beyond creative practices to other fields and related activities. This is partly due to the characteristics of new media, as discussed by Manovich (2001): because today's media are increasingly digital, artists can create, edit and distribute audio, video and image with equal facility. Prior to the digital era, these fields would have been largely separate pursuits with specialised equipment and training required for each. The increasing accessibility and affordability of technologies for media production has meant that artists are able to engage with multiple forms of media production.

Furthermore, the online space has led to a 'flattening out' of outlets for musicians, as discussed in the Foreword of this volume. Whereas promotion and distribution may previously have relied on many geographically distinct local networks of television, radio and print, as well as a distinct music press, a smaller number of globalised outlets—YouTube, Twitter, Facebook, Instagram, and others—are now a significant part of the landscape. Crucially, these outlets are not music-specific, but are generalised platforms for reaching consumers. Artists in today's music environment develop skills for engaging through these particular platforms—engaging audiences and communicating, producing high-quality audiovisual content, analysing metrics, leveraging advertising and so on. These skills are not unique to the domain of music; they are highly transferable and valuable in other fields.

The industry disruption wrought by the Internet has affected not just the technical skills of today's artist, but also the economic aspect of music careers. Recorded music revenues are steadily decreasing, and streaming has yet to be proven as a sufficient income stream for most artists. Live performance remains viable, but touring can involve significant energy, risk and cost to the artist. Artists need to develop initiative in looking elsewhere for revenue, such as selling merchandise or applying for grants from organisations. Alternative funding models such as crowdfunding (via Kickstarter, GoFundMe or similar services) and patronage/subscription services (through Patreon, Bandcamp or others) are also increasingly used. Even direct artist-to-fan engagement provides a space in which to develop ideas and to potentially remove some of the artist 'risk' as some of the financial risk is devolved. Devolving risk through crowdfunding therefore offers the potential for 'testing' creativity both in verification as to the level of funding generated and in the 'success' of the resultant artefact/performance. There are the added benefits of not recouping production costs or advances as well. Each of these funding strategies, however, requires the artist to possess small business skills such as project management and planning, developing a budget, sustainability and innovation; skills that deserve a place in music education and other career development programs.

The new artist is therefore in possession of a wide range of skills beyond musical ability alone. In this context, artists are no longer just music producers or performers; they are independent media producers, with a diverse set of abilities that can be applied to and beyond the music industries. It would, however, be futile to describe the exact skills that a new artist requires; new proficiencies will arise in response to the constantly evolving industries. Above all, new artists need to be agile and resilient enough to adapt to ongoing disruptions caused by technological innovations or changes. While the organisations and services named above are currently widely used, new competitors and changes to these existing services will continue to destabilise the landscape into the future.

Technologies

The role of technology in shaping the new music industries is far-reaching. Before considering what the future may hold for technology, however, it is worth recognising that the 'old' music industry was likewise formed on a particular combination of technologies and economic conditions. Music publishing and copyright developed alongside mass-produced sheet music, itself the result of mass ownership of household pianos. Recorded music led to the rise of labels, which controlled the capital and subsequently manufacturing and distribution processes required for profit generation. The labels' longstanding influence on the industry (and on artists) was contingent on their ownership of capital and the nature of recording technology at the time. Today, technology has refigured the popular music landscape once again.

There are several points about technology and its future impact on the music industries worth making here. First, the accessibility of fans to artists (and vice versa) within the new circular model of artist careers is made possible through the new entities—Internet service providers and web services—which mediate this interaction. Thus, although disintermediation is occurring to an extent, there is always a mediating presence with the potential to affect the fan–artist relationship. Although services such as Facebook offer the impression of a direct connection, it is worth remembering that both artists and fans are subject to Facebook's terms of service, user interface and program algorithms. When using a third-party service, a level of control is ceded; this can be detrimental, as demonstrated when Facebook adjusted its algorithm in 2012, serving up more paid posts to end users (Ogilvy and Mather, 2012). Likewise, use of these services entails agreeing to set terms, including remuneration; this issue was behind Taylor Swift's well-publicised catalogue withdrawal from Spotify in 2014 (Linshi, 2014). While the increased closeness between artist and fan permitted by these services has led to new opportunities for artists (such as one-on-one interactions, crowdfunding and the like), it is worth recognising that this relationship is mediated by third-party entities, and that it is well to be circumspect about the long-term benefits of these services.

Live performance is another area that has been greatly changed by technology. Prior to the Internet, live performance would correspond to a (usually) paid gig in a live music venue to an audience. Such performances are frequently used as an opportunity to sell merchandise, a comparatively profitable area for performing musicians. Today however, live performance—and the definition of 'live'—has changed dramatically (Keith, Hughes, Crowdy, Morrow, & Evans, 2014). New performance technologies are becoming more established, and can make certain performers stand out (see Hughes, 2014, 2015a, 2015b); Ed Sheeran's use of looping technologies is one example (see also Hughes, 2015a), while other performers use more complex set-ups involving Ableton Live or other software, merging performance with pre-recorded material. Artists are also able to 'perform' to audiences in various non-musical ways through social media, using video, text or image. Music performances can also be recorded and uploaded to a video or music-sharing service, such as Spotify's *Spotify Sessions*. In addition, musicians can take advantage of live-streaming technology such as Twitter's Periscope, UStream or Livestream to broadcast a performance in real time. In the latest development, fans will soon be able to buy merchandise while streaming music via Spotify, in an online simulacrum of the concert experience (Spotify Artists Services, 2016). Each of these approaches shows how technology has advanced and changed 'live performance' as a concept.

A third observation revolves around the way music production technology has shifted the role of musical skill. Whereas, in the earliest days of recorded music, the recorded artefact consisted of a fairly straightforward recording of a live performance, the recording studio has long been used to create effects and results that are not possible in a live setting—double-tracking, editing, comping and, most recently, pitch and rhythm correction, to name several. A recurring theme in our research was the divide between artists who can perform live, and those who lack performance ability. As technologies for music production and for altering recorded audio become increasingly widespread and accessible for artists, it is worth questioning whether musical 'skill' in the traditional sense—that is, technical proficiency with an instrument or voice—is still relevant in popular music. Certainly, in some instances sample libraries and software plug-ins (such as Antares' Auto-Tune) allow artists with varying degrees of instrumental skill to produce music (see also Hughes, 2015b). To achieve seemingly credible results, however, a level of musical proficiency, performativity, carefully applied technology and creative ability would still be necessary. Furthermore, as mentioned above, production technology (such as triggering samples) is now commonly used in live performance. Today's artists are increasingly able to frame performance in a way that suits their own level of ability, assisted by technology.

It should also be said that any discussion of the future of technology in regard to artist careers needs to recognise the diversity of genres, subcultures and niches across artistry and related industries. Each musical niche will have its own audience, and a particular set of technologies suited to it. Some artists may be able to eschew many online technologies and build an audience primarily through live performances, while others may not perform 'live' at all. Nonetheless, by recognising the ever-changing entities and technologies present within the music industries, artists can form educated career pathways.

The Future of Business

This volume has proposed several models of career development for artists in the music industries. As we have seen, types of artistry can be illustrated on a continuum of creativity (Madden & Bloom, 2001) (see Fig. 1.1, Chapter 1) and are free to choose their artistic endeavour. Artists also exist, to some extent, on a continuum of business skills. We have therefore highlighted that for all career models, grounding in business principles (including financial, accounting tax and so on) is beneficial. Featured along the continuum are 'advanced' marketing, audience outreach and digital strategies to varying degrees. What is certain in the digital economy is that artists will be affected by the future of business in the digital age.

Even the DIY model, and the way in which it is facilitated by new technologies, has a place within the corporate businesses of the future. While it may be seen to rely on soft business skills (career dependent) that lie outside the scope and interests of traditional music business entities, the DIY model is attractive to numerous online platforms that are commercialising more and more content. Facebook, Twitter, Youtube, WhatsApp, Google, Soundcloud, Bandcamp, Music Glue and many others are all entities that derive economic benefit from the aggregate of the artists and many other people who use new technologies to pursue artistic creativities through the DIY model.

While the DIY model may or may not be used by people who desire to pursue professional careers as artists, it is reasonable to assume the 360 model and the Entrepreneur model will be used in the future by artists who desire to build professional careers in music that involve both soft and hard creativities. However, the fragility of such careers means that artists may well cycle through the DIY model, the Entrepreneur model and the 360 model and then go back to operating via the DIY model. While this may cause issues relating to self-esteem for artists who 'over-identify' (Hesmondhalgh & Baker, 2011, p. 141) with their professional work, it is important to note that there are many benefits that can be derived from participating in music which have significant implications for the wellbeing and development of future artists.

For those who desire to pursue careers as professional, or semi-professional artists, and who seek to break new ground through the innovation and invention stemming from their creative endeavours, many of the old binaries that informed music business discourse (such as independent versus major labels, creativity versus commerce, selling out or buying in) will arguably continue to lose their rigidity in the future business of music. This is because we anticipate an increasing fluidity in terms of artists' use of the career development Models 1 through 3. An artist may be signed to a record label under the 360 model in one geographic territory, while operating through the Entrepreneur model in another. And while longitudinally an artist may start out by operating under a DIY model, then develop their creative practice and investment opportunities through the Entrepreneur model, they may be able to demonstrate to potential investors that they are achieving exponential growth in some form or fashion. They may then begin working with a record label (major or independent) through the 360 model in order to further build their career. We envisage that startup methodologies and approaches will evolve with alarming speed. The new artist will need to be aware of trends within business cycles, as new formations take root and others are ruled out. Moving to a more extreme position, creative businesses might be further automated if artificial intelligence (AI) (see Halal, 2015, p. 57) is engaged to assist artists in their career development efforts. Therefore the question of the automation of—at least some of—the components of artist management service provision and music business development through the use of AI may well in future become an area for development and research.

EDUCATION AND ADVOCACY

In the previous chapter, we posited that multiple creativities (musical and business related) are core to the new artist. We also posited a multidimensional approach to popular music education so as to best cater to multi-platform creativities, and the multi-distribution and production channels now proliferating the industries. We have identified that popular music education needs to reflect the convergence between business operations and the artist. In light of our research findings, we have carefully considered how best to train students for their individual[1] career trajectories within the new music industries. In research that investigated the ways in which popular musicians learn, Green (2002) identified that the musicians in her study supported popular music education. There was, however, some concern expressed in relation to the potential restriction in formal education of musical 'spontaneity' (Green, 2002, p. 176). Much spontaneity stems from adaptability, a skill that may be explored through the creativities that underpin our discussion in the previous chapter.

We have not simply argued that the popular music landscape has changed and is constantly evolving; we have also offered considerations and strategies for navigating through the landscape that is relevant to the artist, to the related practitioner/strategist, to the music educator and/or to the music manager. We have offered a theoretical and practical discussion of what is new from an education perspective (such as the artist–business convergence), highlighted areas for concern (such as duty of care) and have of course identified areas for opportunity (such as the significance of the direct artist-to-fan relationship). We posit that as the popular music landscape continues to change, strategies such as the 'agile-lean startup' methodology will be adapted to quickly test market and/or business assumptions. In this way, we have tapped into the 'agile' trend in order to further differentiate our research and this volume, and to make the argument that it is this agility (together with multiple creativities and versatility) that ultimately leads to discovery and sustainability within the industries.

If the role of tertiary music education is to prepare students for the music industries, then what specifically prepares students for entry into tertiary popular music programs? While it was beyond the original scope of our project, it is relevant to discuss music education in Australia more broadly in an attempt to address this question. At the 2015 national conferences of both the Australian Society for Music Education[2] and the Australian National Association of Teachers of Singing Limited,[3] advocacy for music education in Australian schools was a recurrent theme and concern as music (and singing) have been marginalised to being one of five artforms in school curriculum – Dance, Drama, Media Arts, Music and Visual Arts (Australian Curriculum, Assessment and Reporting Authority, n.d.). This is despite the fact that neuroscience identifies that musical learning has the potential to positively affect brain development (see Herholz & Zatorre, 2012) and a range of associated skills as Wan and Shlaug (2010) highlighted:

> Music training in children, when commenced at a young age, results in improved cognitive performance and possibly the development of exceptional musical abilities such as absolute pitch. (Wan & Shlaug, 2010, p. 574)

Engagement in the new industries (such as through a range of technologies) has much to offer school curriculum content in terms of accessibility, participation and socio-cultural relevance. Over twenty years ago, Negroponte (1995) was also espousing the potential merits of digital technologies:

> The use of computers to learn music at a very young age is a perfect example of the benefit computers provide by offering a complete range of entry points. The computer does not limit musical access to the gifted child. Musical games, sound data tapes, and the intrinsic manipulability of digital audio are just a few of the many means through which a child can experience music. The visually inclined child may even wish to invent ways to see it. (Negroponte, 1995, pp. 222–223)

While we endorse the inclusion of, and access to, music studies throughout school education and are concerned over its marginalisation, it is highly advantageous to also include contemporary content and technologies when teaching music in schools. From a young age, aspects of the new industries (such as looping technologies,[4] Ableton Push[5]) can be used to foster musical creativities, exploration of, and interest in, musical endeavours as Barr (2014) noted:

> Looping is one of the easiest, yet most powerful ways to leverage technology in the music classroom and is a great way to improvise and compose in real time, and share and collaborate in your classroom… There are a number of forms of looping—in this case I am talking about recording some audio, having it play and repeat over and over, allowing you to record additional layers of sound on top.

Such strategies can redress the potential hierarchy associated with much traditional musical learning and its potential isolation (such as in lengthy practice hours). We by no means intend to negate the relevance of formal instrumental learning and its resultant skill development and prowess.

Rather, we advocate for traditional musical concepts (such as melody, harmony, structure) and skill development (such as aural, compositional, improvisational) to also be explored in collective and less traditional ways.

One of the primary challenges facing popular music education is the speed at which the field changes and adapts to meet technological developments, artistic and creative opportunities, business and market demands. Throughout this volume, we have provided an overview of the opportunities and challenges facing artists in the early twenty-first century. While there is relevance to the Australian market, we are also discussing global phenomena that transverse geographical boundaries. At the outset, our premise was that digital disruption has changed the music industries and related practices globally, and in correlation with this we have identified *new means of musical learning* that need to be developed and adopted. The detailed 'on-the-ground' analysis, models, considerations and strategies that we provide through this volume are therefore relevant everywhere.

The 'New' Industries

This volume has attempted to provide some concrete directions for artists in the new music industries to follow. It has developed models that outline the changed landscape within the sector. It has been grounded in practice, in the everyday situation of artists and industry practitioners. And it has shown, that, despite the disruption, there is tremendous discovery occurring. Artists have a power now they never knew before, and the industry is scrambling to take stock of the changes. There are numerous industry professionals—with job titles and descriptors that are totally alien to the traditional music industry—ready to assist in the development of promising artistic creativity. Likewise, there are artists willing to take on their own business-related risks and strategies. In relation to the sale of *Whispers Two* (Rosenberg, 2015), for example, Passenger commented on the accompanying booklet/sleeve (the following excerpt is as written):

> i have no idea if we will raise a lot of money but i have learnt that success comes from making an effort and taking risks and the only way of ensuring failure is not to try

Yet all of these opportunities have occurred in response to technology, and future artists need to be aware of this. In 1995 Nicholas Negroponte prophesised that 'everything that can be digitised, will be digitised'. But what he did not predict was that everything that could be connected would be connected.[6] As we head deeper into the 'Internet of Things', where between 50 and 100 billion machines will be connected, huge changes to the fabric of artistic endeavour will no doubt continue to evolve. Artists need to be technologically adept, to be agile and to embrace the possibility that these changes constantly pose. At the same time, as traditional media move online, as video games (both serious and recreational) subsume film and popular music for total value creation, opportunities for musical artists continue to arise and develop. The new artist needs to be adept at discovering these opportunities. There will be much to read about disruption and future (as yet unseen) disruptive technologies, but as we have seen, with all such developments there are untold discoveries to be made. Wearable technology is beginning to gain a foothold in consumer consciousness; what happens when artists manage to distribute their product via such technologies? At the heart of all such postulations is a strong creative product—music that people would want to wear, for instance—and acute business acumen. The new musical industries present no shortcuts, and no substitute for hard work. Yet there are models of operation, and levels of understanding, that will provide advantage to artists willing to discovery the new territories.

Throughout this book, we have highlighted the versatility required of artists in the digital music economy as they navigate their way through the multi-industry landscape. After first outlining the primary reasons why many twentieth-century popular music practices and assumptions are now outdated, the abilities and skills of the new artist are addressed through citing and analysing specific practice examples. As such, our research findings and the models presented in this volume are crucial to understanding, navigating and succeeding in the new musical industries. We hope that this volume, among others, may help readers understand the current state of the play, as well as prepare for future eventualities as they occur.

We have posited our book as a research volume with detailed findings and exciting provocations to expand our understanding of music industries from a confined, traditional base to a digitally networked hybrid. Many of our participants were digital content creators and curators, not simply artists. This represents an industry-wide study, far broader than music practices. It is, therefore, highly relevant internationally. This is not a 'how-to' book, but rather a 'what's happening' account of explorations of the new spaces and practices, both positive and negative, that exist within the popular music industries. It is time to look beyond the disruption; to discover.

Notes

1. The use of 'individual' in this context relates to the particular trajectory undertaken rather than referring to the individual artist per se.
2. 'Music: Educating for Life', Australian Society for Music Education (ASME) XXth National Conference, 30 September–2 October, 2015, Adelaide, Australia.
3. 'Singing Futures: Pedagogies Practices and the Digital Age', National Conference of the Australian National Association of Teachers of Singing Limited (ANATS), 24–27 September 2015, Hobart, Australia.
4. Looping technologies include software and/or hardware that enable simultaneous playback and recording.
5. See *Push: Music at your fingertips*, Accessed on 29 January 2016 at https://www.ableton.com/en/push/?gclid=COTrp_O3nMsCFRYIvAodFmkNYQ.
6. For more see the blogsite inma, http://www.inma.org/blogs/mobile-tablets/post.cfm/6-quotes-from-digital-leaders-that-point-to-the-digital-revolution-s-future, accessed 29 February 2016.

References

Australian Curriculum, Assessment and Reporting Authority. (n.d.). Introduction. *The Arts*. Retrieved February 29, 2016 from http://www.australiancurriculum.edu.au/the-arts/introduction

Bandura, A. (1997). *Self-efficacy: The exercise of control*. New York: Worth Publishers.

Barr, A. (2014). Introduce technology into your music classroom. *Education Technology Solutions*. Retrieved February 29, 2016, from http://educationtechnologysolutions.com.au/2014/10/31/introduce-technology-into-your-music-classroom/

Green, L. (2002). *How popular musicians learn: A way ahead for music education*. Aldershot, UK/Burlington, USA: Ashgate Publishing Limited.

Halal, B. (2015). Forecasting future disruptions – Strategic change is inevitable. In R. Talwar (Ed.), *The future of business: Critical insights into a rapidly changing world from 60 future thinkers*. London, UK: Fast Future Publishing.

Herholz, S. C., & Zatorre, R. J. (2012). Musical training as a framework for brain plasticity: Behavior, function, and structure. *Neuron, 76*(2), 486–502.

Hesmondhalgh, D., & Baker, S. (2011). *Creative labour: Media work in three cultural industries*. London: Routledge.

Hughes, D. (2014). 'Truthful' representation in the technological processing of the singing voice. In M. Angelucci & C. Caines (Eds.), *Voice / Presence / Absence – Media object 2*. Sydney: UTS ePress. Available online: http://epress.lib.uts.edu.au/books/voicepresenceabsence

Hughes, D. (2015a). Technological pitch correction: controversy, contexts and considerations. *Journal of Singing, 71*(5), 587–594.

Hughes, D. (2015b). Technologized and autonomized vocals in cotemporary popular musics. *Journal of Music Technology and Education, 8*(2), 163–182.

Keith, S., Hughes, D., Crowdy, D., Morrow, G., & Evans, M. (2014). Offline and online: Liveness in the Australian music industries. In V. Sarafian and R. Findlay (Eds.). *Civilisations: The State of the Music Industries, 13*, 221–241.

Kelley, D., & Kelley, T. (2013). *Creative confidence: Unleashing the creative potential in us all*. London, UK: HarperCollins Publishers.

Linshi, J. (2014, November 3). Here's why Taylor Swift pulled her music from spotify. *Time.com*. Retrieved February 11, 2016, from http://time.com/3554468/why-taylor-swift-spotify/

Madden, C., & Bloom, T. (2001). Advocating creativity. *International Journal of Cultural Policy, 7*(3), 409–436.

Manovich, L. (2001). *The language of new media*. Cambridge, MA: MIT Press.

Negroponte, N. (1995). *Being digital*. New York: Alfred A. Knoph.

Negus, K. (1996). *Popular music in theory: An introduction*. Cambridge, UK: Polity Press.

Ogilvy and Mather. (2012, September 25). *Facebook algorithmic change to decrease reach on brand page posts*. Retrieved February 11, 2016, from https://social.ogilvy.com/facebook-algorithmic-change-to-decrease-reach-on-brand-page-posts/

Rosenberg, M. (2015). *Whispers II* [Book accompanying CD]. Black Crow Records.

Spotify Artist Services. (2016). *Welcome to spotify for artists!* Retrieved February 11, 2016, from http://www.spotifyartists.com/welcome-to-spotify-for-artists/

Throsby, D. (2002). *The music industry in the new millennium: Global and local perspectives*. Unpublished paper prepared for the Division of Arts and Cultural Enterprise, UNESCO, Paris.

Wan, C., & Shlaug, G. (2010). Music making as a tool for promoting brain plasticity across the life span. *The Neuroscientist, 16*(5), 566–577.

Welch, C. (2003). *Peter Grant: The man who Led Zeppelin*. London, UK: Omnibus Press.

Index

A
Apple Music, vi, 71, 76
artist entrepreneurship. *See* entrepreneurship
artistry, 86, 98, 99, 108, 109, 124
artist safety, 82, 83, 91–3, 111, 113
artistic creativity. *See* creativity
artist success. *See* success
See also WHS
audience, vii, ix–x, 2, 4, 5, 6, 9, 10, 18, 22, 26–7, 28, 38, 48, 65, 68, 69–70, 72, 73, 75–6, 77, 91, 121, 124
authenticity, 24, 38, 43, 56, 66, 67, 69–70, 71
authorship, 63, 64, 66–70, 71, 77
self-social, 66, 67, 75
sociocultural, 66, 75, 76

B
Bandcamp, 48, 51, 121, 124
bicycle wheel analogy, 31–2

booking, x, 28, 48, 49, 50, 54, 104
bottom up and top down paradigms, 29
brand, branding, 38, 39, 41, 42–4, 47, 49, 52–3, 56, 67, 70, 71, 82, 98, 99, 103, 109
busking, 75–6

C
career models, 14, 20–6, 31–2, 53–4. *See also* 360-degree (360) career model, DIY career model, entrepreneur career model
career sustainability, 20, 21, 23, 31, 48, 85–6, 88, 99, 102
career trajectories, 11, 17, 20, 71, 81, 98, 113n3, 126
CDBaby, 48
circular career model, 17, 28–30, 31, 38, 41, 70, 118, 119, 122
collaboration, 1, 68, 69, 71–3, 75, 77, 87, 99, 100
competition, viii, 57, 86, 108

Note: Page numbers with 'n' denote notes.

copyright, ix, x, 7, 18, 64, 65, 81, 84–5, 111, 113, 122
copyright collection, 65, 84–5, 113
Countdown (TV show), 46
covers, 10, 64, 73–5, 77
  live, 75
  online, 73–4, 75
co-writing, co-writes, 63, 69, 71–3
creativities, 9–11, 64, 98–9, 100, 105, 118, 124, 125–6
  musical, 8, 37–56n3, 65, 67, 70, 71, 73, 75, 76–7, 101–2, 117, 127
  non-musical, 70
creativity
  hard creativity, 10–11, 18, 31, 37, 38, 40, 41–2, 45, 124
  hard versus soft creativity, 10–11
  paramusical, 77
  in songwriting, 65, 71, 99, 111
  in strategies for self-managed artists, 89, 102, 104
  strong versus weak creativity, 10–11
Cyrus, Miley, 90

D
Darwin, Charles, v, vi, ix
digital disruption, iv, viii, x, 2, 7, 11, 12, 82, 128
direct-to-fan, 48, 50, 52, 53, 54, 55
discovery, vi, ix, 6–7, 13, 28, 71, 126, 128, 129
disruption, iv, 1, 3, 6–7, 11, 13, 21, 22, 27, 54–5, 120, 121, 128, 129. *See also* digital disruption
DIY (Do-It-Yourself), 8, 49, 68, 70, 82, 85, 87, 88, 101–2, 103
DIY career model, 6, 18, 20, 23–6, 31, 38, 40, 51, 53, 120, 124–5. *See also* DIY

E
employability, 100–1
Enter Shikari, 50, 51
entrepreneur career model, 18, 20, 22–3, 24, 26, 27, 31, 38, 40, 53, 101, 120, 124–5
entrepreneurship, 6, 27, 99–102, 104, 107, 111
  hypothesis-driven, 46, 51

F
Facebook, vi, 43, 47, 48, 68, 70, 72, 120, 122, 124. *See also* social media
fanbase, ix, 18, 48, 50
fan data, 49, 50, 53, 54
fans/fandom, viii, ix, 4, 6, 9, 22, 23, 28–30, 41, 47–8, 49–50, 51–3, 54, 56, 68, 69, 71, 72, 73, 87, 120, 122, 123
financial risk. *See* risk

G
gatekeepers, vii, viii, ix, 28, 29, 46
Gentlemen of the Road, 52, 53
gig. *See* live performance
Gotye (Wouter "Wally" de Backer), 44–5, 73
government funding, 105
grants. *See* government funding
group creativity. *See* shared creativity

H
health and wellbeing, 11, 84, 91, 110, 113
legislation, 83
house concerts/parlour gigs, 53

I

image, 43, 56, 67, 82, 88, 89–90, 101, 108. *See also* brand
I Manage My Own Music, 104
innovation in career development, 37, 40, 56n1, 106, 121, 125
insecurity
  income, 46, 99
  work, 99
insurance, 110, 111, 113
Internet, vi, ix, 7, 21, 29, 55, 64, 65, 72–3, 120, 121, 122
label career model. *See* 360-degree (360) career model

L

lean startup, 38, 39, 46, 56, 126
liberalism, 23–4
linear career model, 17, 28–31, 53, 118
live performance, x, 5, 49, 53, 75, 83, 85, 121, 122–3, 124
  and career sustainability, 82, 88
  and covers. *See* covers, live
  and oversupply of musicians, 88
lockout laws, 5

M

management/managers, 11, 12, 22, 23, 26, 27, 28, 31, 38, 41, 42, 43, 46, 48, 49, 51, 54, 55, 56, 67, 68, 69, 70, 72, 81, 86, 87, 89, 90, 92, 98, 101–2, 103–6, 111–13, 118, 120
media production
  technologies, 120
methodology. *See* research methodology

merchandise, merch, x, 18, 38, 42, 44, 45, 48, 49, 51, 52, 68, 103, 121, 122–3
Minchin, Tim, 76
Mumford and Sons, 50, 52–3, 57n8
music business in education.
  See music education, and music business
music education
  and brain development, 126
  and music business, 98, 99, 101, 111, 112
  in traditional music education, 98, 127
Music Glue, 49–52, 53, 54, 55, 57n7, 103, 124
music production technologies, 68, 108, 123
music subscription services, 4, 19–20
musical creativities. *See* creativities
MVP (minimum viable product), 23, 32n6, 38, 40, 45, 53

N

neo-Fordism and post-Fordism, 17
neoliberalism, 17
  in tertiary education, 100
networking, 82, 85, 87–8
new artist, the, 117–30
new media skills, 120
non-musical creativities.
  See creativities
novelty, 10, 37, 38, 40, 41–2, 44, 46, 47, 74

P

Passenger, 75–6, 77n3, 78n4
performance. *See* live performance
physical distribution, vii

physical injury, 93. *See also* WHS
physical media, 48, 71
piracy, vi, 3
pivot, 38, 42, 56, 56n2
popular music education, 97–113, 125–6, 128
professional, professionalism, 6, 8, 82, 84, 100, 104, 113n3, 125, 128
promotion/promoters, x, 25, 28, 49, 50, 52, 54–5, 67, 91, 120
prosumer, 70
publishing, 12, 18–19, 22, 24, 44, 72, 122

R
radio, vi, vii, 46, 47, 57n6, 70
recording industry, 20, 22
and reactive business practices, 18, 26, 28, 29, 30
record labels, 6, 17–18, 21, 23, 24, 26, 28, 29, 32n2, 41, 55, 57n9, 68, 70, 101, 118, 125
research methodology, 11–13
revenue streams, 4, 5, 18–20, 21–2, 68, 71, 77, 86, 88, 93, 103, 111
risk
devolving/externalising risk, 17, 22, 26, 101, 105–6, 107, 121
financial risk, 18, 26, 32n1, 38, 101, 105–6, 107, 121
royalty collection. *See* copyright collection

S
self-employment, 85, 99, 100
self-social authorship. *See* authorship
shared creativity, 103–5
Sia Furler, 8
small and large business entities, 27

social media, vi, 9, 24, 26, 40, 41, 43, 47, 50, 55, 64, 67, 68, 69, 72–3, 76, 103, 108, 123
sharing, 72
sociocultural authorship. *See* authorship
soft creativity. *See* creativity
song, vi, vii, viii, x, 18–19, 45, 63–6, 70–1, 74, 75–6, 77, 108
Spotify, vi, viii, 3–4, 27, 68–9, 72, 76, 88, 122, 123. *See also* music subscription services
startups, 45–7, 51, 125, 126
and artist careers, 23, 32, 38–40, 41, 42, 52, 53, 54, 56
the lean startup, 38, 39, 46, 56
streaming, vi, 3–4, 5, 18–20, 21, 23, 68–9, 71–2, 77, 83, 86, 88, 93, 103, 111, 121, 123. *See also* music subscription services
subcultural capital, 38, 43, 56
subscription services. *See* music subscription services
substance use/abuse, 83–4, 93
success, 1, 2, 8–9, 11, 27, 39, 40, 41–2, 51–2, 85, 90, 99, 120, 121
suicide, 83
synchronisation/sync, 5, 8, 19, 44, 68–9, 71, 74, 77

T
technology, 1, 6, 11, 64, 67–71, 77, 88, 101, 108, 120, 122–4, 127, 128–9
in artist careers, 122, 124
and live performance, 122–3, 124
and musical skill, 68, 123
360 (rapper), 84
360-degree (360) career model, 18, 20, 21–3, 27, 31, 32n5, 51, 55, 120, 124–5
ticketing, 48, 49, 50, 52, 53, 54, 55

Topspin, 48–9
touring, x, 49–50, 53, 87, 92, 121
traditional music education.
    See music education
triple j, 44, 57n6, 70

V
validated learning, 32n6, 47, 48, 54
visual design/visual marketing, 43, 45

W
weak creativity. *See* creativity
WHS (Workplace Health and Safety),
    85, 91–2
    and irregular hours, 91–2
    and safety checks, 92

Y
YouTube, v, vi, vii, 24, 25, 43, 45, 48,
    68, 69, 71, 72, 73, 74, 120, 124

Druck:
Canon Deutschland Business Services GmbH
im Auftrag der KNV-Gruppe
Ferdinand-Jühlke-Str. 7
99095 Erfurt